5 Loaves and 2 Fishes

First published April 2017

ISBN 9781545300916

All scripture quoted is from the NIV unless otherwise stated

Artwork by Becci Tamaklo

© New Hope 2017

Five loaves and two fishes

Preface

A year ago we spoke to a class of Ghanaian orphans. They were so motivated to make their lives count, but they were only too aware that they had not been given the best starts in life. We encouraged them that God can do great things with a life - any life. But there is a pre-condition. It is simply this. He wants us to surrender all we are and all we have to him. No matter whether we believe our life to be of value or not.

The thing is that to God, all lives are of immense value. But we may take a long time to grasp that. What I mean is that in our enthusiasm to serve God, we can easily believe that God needs what we have to offer. Maybe natural gifts, maybe energy, maybe skills or maybe spiritual gifts and experience. We can falsely believe he needs us for years.

Eventually and inevitably as we walk with the Master, something happens. We realise that actually we have very little to offer, and that God doesn't need anything we have! But our wonderful Father loves us, and wants to draw us into the family business. So what can we give? How can we contribute? The boy with the loaves and fishes gives us such a great example. What he gave was not much, but it sparked one of the most amazing miracles in the Bible.

Five loaves and two fishes

Over the last 40 years as Myra and I have learned to give him the little we have - our loaves and fishes, God has taken us into many miraculous situations, often without any sense of being in control on our part. So now we want to share the journey. And the fun! We hope it helps you to believe God will use you.

If you have any inclination to serve God in mission and ministry, either at home or overseas, this book has been written for you. You may never leave the shores of your land, or even the town where you grew up. It doesn't matter. The God of mission wants us to start where we are, with what we have. He wants us to offer our loaves and fishes, even though they seem so inadequate.

We tell our stories as honestly as we are able. We look back at many and laugh! God has taken us through some experiences we never expected.

But we earnestly believe it was only because we offered what little we had. Our prayer is this book encourages you to do just that.

We are joint authors, both of us describing our own specific experiences. In order to avoid constant confusion, we use the word 'I' throughout much of the book. But to help you to understand which of us is

Five loaves and two fishes

writing, each chapter is marked with the main author's name.

John & Myra Sloan, April 2017

Five loaves and two fishes

Contents

Preface

Introduction

Maps

Chapter 1 Reluctant disciples

Chapter 2 Passports please

Chapter 3 Church Planting to Medical Mission

Chapter 4 Learning to trust God on Mission

Chapter 5 Getting serious

Chapter 6 Taking bigger risks

Chapter 7 More of the Philippines

Chapter 8 Africa!

Chapter 9 Deeper into Africa

Chapter 10 Francophone Africa at last

Chapter 11 We never imagined this!

Chapter 12 The God of miracles

Endnotes

Five loaves and two fishes

Introduction - John

There are very few events which are recorded in all four gospels. The feeding of the 5,000 is the one miracle, apart from the resurrection, that is found in all of them[i]. It occurs at an interesting time in the disciple's development. Jesus started with recruits, who rapidly became observers. Probably fascinated observers! But he clearly wanted them to start to do things themselves. So this miracle occurred at a stage where Jesus had begun to transition the disciples from observers to do-ers and it is a little while into their training. They had already been sent out in pairs on their first mission alone, and they had come back excited about what had happened. Around this time a horrific event occurred when Jesus' cousin, John the Baptist, was beheaded. Jesus decided they all needed to get away in order to get some rest So they went to a quiet place.

If you have visited Lake Galilee you will know it is not large - around 20km long and 10km wide, and it was not difficult for the crowds to track where Jesus and his team had gone. Going by boat was playing catch-me, as Jesus and his disciples were visible from the shore. Luke records they went to Bethsaida, at the north eastern tip of the lake[ii]. Even today it is a rural spot, close to the grassy hill a few miles from where the sermon on the mount had taken place. It is close to

Five loaves and two fishes

the eastern shore where the pigs had drowned. They went by boat, but the crowds hurried around by foot and were waiting for them. I have been to that exact spot. They would have been easy to stalk. And once they arrived, there was a convergence of expectations. The majority wanted healing and release from oppression[iii]. Some simply wanted to hear this magnificent man who spoke with passion and seemed to have inside knowledge about the "Kingdom of God" as he kept calling it. Some of the religious heavy weights were determined to add his new "heresies" to their bourgeoning list of his previous alleged misdemeanours. The disciples wanted to chatter. Meanwhile Jesus had experienced a personal tragedy, and wanted time alone. But scripture records he saw the crowds for what they really were - sheep without a shepherd[iv]. And he had compassion for them, despite his own needs.

You can't choose the time when people are ready and open - they choose it. This is hard for our western minds to grasp, as we are so accustomed to booking a slot for people. Our African friends say "a black man has time but no clock, while a white man has a clock but no time!" But perhaps we need to adjust and learn from this event in Jesus' life. Years later Paul, the murdering terrorist, transformed into a servant of God, wrote this in I Corinthians 9:19 "Though I am free and belong to no man, I make myself a slave to everyone,

Five loaves and two fishes

to win as many as possible". Being a slave to people means we let *them* dictate terms.

Being available for people is something we might not be good at. But here we see Jesus demonstrating it so fully. He could be flexible, jettison his personal wishes and change his plan. And so "he welcomed them and spoke to them about the Kingdom of God"[v].

I have been a Christian over 40 years, and I can remember the small number of times I have heard people teach on the Kingdom of God. And yet Jesus did it all the time. In fact most of his teaching was about the Kingdom. He spoke of it over 40 times. He spoke about it for hours, and kept everyone riveted. Maybe it was because what he brought was so different. Maybe it was because he had actually experienced it in reality. There was mercy instead of judgement. There was grace instead of severity. There was joy instead of sadness. Most of all there was a fresh start for any that wanted it, no matter what had gone before.

I am sure it was the desire to understand the amazing grace Jesus projected that captivated the crowds. In this impromptu session (which most of his exchanges were), he also healed those who needed healing. Again, their needs determined his agenda. I can't imagine him explaining to some sick people "you

Five loaves and two fishes

need to wait on God", or "your illness is God's will" or even "God must be doing something only He understands". Of course we are used to such language because the power we see in our lives is a bit limited compared to his. Having said that, he did not heal everyone in the land, and it seems he worked in union with Father God's direction. That is certainly something we need to get better at.

Several hours passed and late in the afternoon the 12 disciples came to him. I picture them having a bit of a union meeting, then trying to get his attention. Maybe Peter was gesticulating, showing his characteristic bluster. Maybe young John, always at Jesus' side, was gently poking him. However they did it, when they got his attention, their message was profound, heart-felt and practical: "Get rid of this lot". These were the excited missionaries who had returned from up-country with miracle stories. But they had not absorbed much of their master's style when it came to being available, loving, serving or meeting need.

At this stage Jesus makes it clear the disciples really were in training when he said to the 12 "You give them something to eat"[vi]. You could have heard a pin drop! There were 5,000 men present. This was not a sexist observation, it was just the way the culture of that time counted crowds. So there were probably at least 12,000 people there, with women and children

Five loaves and two fishes

included. Maybe 15,000 in total. Various rational comments followed, such as eight months wages not buying enough bread for each one to have a bite. Maybe Judas commented how Jesus always made a miscalculation. Of course, much of what they said was probably true. Their problem was they were just looking at the situation and not looking at the *author* of the situation.

Scripture is full of examples of people who see the facts as they are, but they fail to see the maker of the universe. They fail to understand that with God, all things are possible. As a result they say the impossible is simply impossible. The Old Testament spies, sent out by Moses are an example[vii]. Chosen from the highest ranks of the 12 tribes they were the best. They were the select warriors. They all saw the facts as they were. What they saw was that the promised land could not be taken because of the massive fighters who lived there. But only Joshua and Caleb saw the plan that God had. They understood God had given the land to them. They wanted to go forward, but were outvoted. And as a result the democratic process held them in suspended animation for the next 40 years.

David is another example. King Saul and the Israelites were surrounded by the Philistines and their champion, Goliath[viii]. He was formidable. At over 9ft

Five loaves and two fishes

tall he carried armour that was legendary. His spear was like "a weaver's beam". A weaver made cloth to a standard width, probably 6 feet wide so that one-piece garments could be made. So including side pieces it was perhaps 8 feet long. The diameter of the beam had to be sufficient to prevent flexing and is thought to have been around two and a half inches. Then it was tipped with an iron head of 600 shekels weight. This puts the total weight around 9-10kg. Of course we could lift one, but for most of us throwing it more than 3-4metres would not be possible!

Now David had only just been anointed by Samuel[ix], and he knew there was a mantle of anointing resting on him. Though he had probably considered it a misfortune to have been a shepherd on the hills day after day, God had intended it to be a training. He had regularly defended the flock from wild animals using a simple sling and stones. And on this day all he had to say was "Who is this uncircumcised Philistine that he should defy the armies of the living God?" And with that, he locked into God's purpose, ignoring the odds, and believed the impossible could become possible. He dismissed the offer of armour - he could barely stand up in it because of its weight. He knew God was his armour. Though young, ill-equipped and naive, he slaughtered Goliath with a sling and a smooth stone.

Five loaves and two fishes

We need to see that the mantle of anointing rests also on us. And that means we can see some things happen against all the odds. In Jesus' dealing with us we all start from different places. But he takes us on similar journeys, and one path is sure. He moves us from being rational thinkers to being what I call 'possibility thinkers'. People who can believe God could actually do something in a seemingly impossible situation. Some of us struggle with this more than others simply because they are hard-wired to be rational. Perhaps we should stop and ask ourselves how we are doing as 'possibility thinkers'?

Back to Jesus, the crowd and the doubting disciples. On this particular day Jesus sees their problem, but decides to move them further down this faith journey. He asks "How many loaves do you have? Go and see"[x]. This is the beginning of miracles. Go and see. Take a look. Start by thinking about doing what your head tells you is probably a waste of time.

Exactly what happened next is only recorded in one gospel. Andrew piped up "Here is a boy with five small barley loaves and two small fish."[xi]. Note the double use of the word small. It was hardly faith-talk. Then for doubting disciple good measure he added, "How far will that go among so many?"

Five loaves and two fishes

I imagine Jesus realised he had squeezed as much faith out of his 12 as he was going to get on that day. So he took over. He had at least moved them on, and he had other thoughts for the next step in their faith training (such as walking on water). So he ordered that the disciples sat the people in groups of 50. At least they could do that and still feel involved.

I don't really know why he did the groups of 50 thing. But I can guess. Once we went to Bombay as a family. We decided to walk on the beach where people lived in abject poverty. Nearby, over a tall dividing wall, the film stars quaffed champagne, and lived in luxury. Everyone we met urged us not to venture onto the beach. But we had some pillows and blankets we had collected from the previous two weeks spent in a camper van in Australia, and we wanted to give them away. When the crowds saw that there was something good on offer, they almost crushed us. It was disconcerting as our three children were young, in fact 7, 5 and 3 years of age. We should have seated the crowds in groups of 50. There was one young mother, barely 21 years old, with three children. Her young husband had recently died of tuberculosis. She had nothing. It was a joy to be there to provide something small. The beach children all had nits in their hair, but were peppered regularly with DDT by the authorities. Naturally, in due course, the nits became resistant. When we got home a letter

Five loaves and two fishes

came from the head teacher to all the parents. There was an atypical, and very resistant strain of nit which had entered the school. The head and the governors were mystified.

So perhaps Jesus sat the crowd in 50's to avoid a dangerous clamour for food. He took the five loaves and the two fish, and prayed over them. He then broke them into pieces and gave bits to each disciple. I really can't imagine this. At some point the bits became bigger bits. And the fish bits became bigger fish bits. Everything became bites. Then it became a buffet with waiters. Suddenly it was an "all you can eat" supper totally for free. Jesus had the disciples take part in a miracle which minutes earlier they were not remotely ready to contemplate! And furthermore, we see that the distribution was abundant, each having as much as they wanted[xii], with 12 baskets being filled with leftovers.

Abundance is an interesting characteristic of Jesus. I know Christians whose outlook on life is quite severe. They tend to ration everything including joy. But Jesus is not like that. I am sure he started to laugh and laugh when he saw the food going round. And I suspect the disciples slowly joined in. Its the sort of event I would have loved to have watched. If only because it would have been such fun! It must have reminded them of the wedding feast at Cana where the mediocre wine

Five loaves and two fishes

ran out and Jesus turned water into the very best wine. Just out of his loving, abundant heart. They must have laughed on that day too!

On this occasion, when people slowly drifted off, I am sure they returned to their villages and stayed up late, telling the story again and again, each from a unique perspective.

It is an amazing account with many facets for us to appreciate. But as we start describing our journey to you, lets focus on two. Firstly Jesus used the rational-minded unbelieving, reluctant disciples who, basically, wanted to get rid of the crowds and go home. That's great news for us, because Myra and I are very much like that. And we would guess you are much the same.

Secondly, the boy whom Andrew found, made it all possible. His mum had probably given him the loaves and the fish for his food that day. All he had to do was hand his lunch over. It wasn't much. He could also have slinked off, eaten it behind a bush and gone home. But the act of handing it over acted as a fuse which completed a powerful circuit. A momentous miracle occurred. He must have been dumbfounded. I can imagine him stumbling home when it was all over, dizzy with excitement, trying to come to terms with what had happened. I can see him telling the story

Five loaves and two fishes

breathlessly to his mum, then many times over to hundreds more over the years. He had a testimony to tell his friends, children and grandchildren. He probably dined out on the story all his life. Besides this, he gets a mention in the Bible, the world's all-time best seller, and is known about by billions of believers over two millennia. Not bad for a boy who sacrificed one lunch. And it's also great news for us, because in terms of wisdom, strategy, money, resource and time, all Myra and I have is something that equates to a few loaves and fish. And again, we would guess you are much the same.

Revelation 12:11 says "They overcame him_by the blood of the Lamb and by the word of their testimony; they did not love their lives so much as to shrink from death". There are two highly significant principles here. They both relate to kingdom breakthrough, as we only see breakthrough by taking territory away from the evil one. Firstly we see kingdom breakthrough by coming under the blood of the lamb. "I know that" I hear you say.

Secondly, we also need testimony. In other words we have put what we believe into practice, and have a story to tell as a result. Without, we can't see any breakthrough in our own lives, in our marriages, in our families, in our work place or in our community.

Five loaves and two fishes

Putting it simply, that day the boy traded his lunch for a testimony.

The late Jim Elliott wrote "He is no fool who gives what he cannot keep to gain what he cannot lose". We have discovered over the last few decades Jesus will take minimal faith, with scant resource, and if we put it into his hands we trade it for a testimony. And then there is no limit to what he can do. We trust you will be motivated by the same vision.

Five loaves and two fishes

Maps

South America (showing Venezuela, Guyana, Brasil)

Guyana (showing Venezuela, Pomeroon, Georgetown, Bartica, Essiquibo River, Suriname)

Five loaves and two fishes

The Philippines

- Manila
- Dipolog
- Ipil
- Mindanao Island

Five loaves and two fishes

Africa

Uganda

Kenya

Congo Brazzaville

D R Congo

Five loaves and two fishes

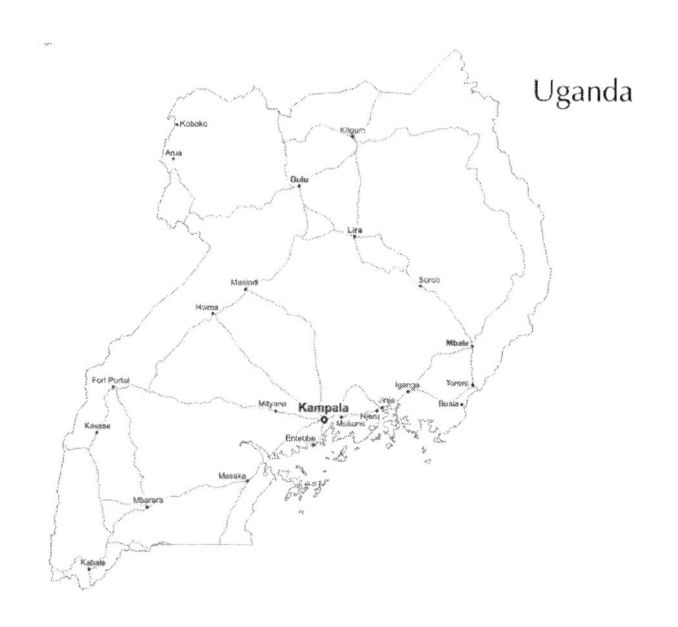

Uganda

Five loaves and two fishes

Five loaves and two fishes

Chapter 1 - Reluctant disciples - John

It was a cold night in February 1975, eighteen months into our medical school training. We had been exposed to the gospel since we had arrived at medical school, but for me it was largely a nuts and bolts theory. It had not really penetrated my heart very deeply. Yes it might all be true, but somehow it was not very compelling.

I had come to accept that Jesus had lived. I understood that he claimed to be one with God, and that his purpose was to rescue me from my sin. And I had come to believe he had probably risen from the dead. Furthermore, I had no difficulty accepting I was not perfect, and yes, I sinned. But it didn't seem that big an issue. The Gospel confronted me with this challenge: God loved me sufficiently to pay the price for my errors by sacrificing Jesus on the cross. It just remained for me to accept this gift of new life. For months I struggled with this, nor wanting to give up any control. This made me miserable, and I considered leaving medical school.

All this had started soon after arriving at Nottingham University Medical School in October 1973. Prior to that, though raised as a Catholic, I was happily irreligious. Some years before I had rejected God as an invention of man. But on arrival at the University I

Five loaves and two fishes

soon met people who called themselves "Christians". As if I was not. After all I was born in the UK. But they pressed me to look at the Bible and try and understand the claims of Jesus.

Within one month I was persuaded that Jesus lived, died and probably had risen from the dead. It was troubling, unsettling and dislocating, all at once. Largely because I saw that surrender to Christ was the inevitable outcome for a believer. And surrender was definitely not in my plan. Quite the opposite.

Myra had started to follow Jesus faithfully but I remained very reluctant. As a 19 year old male I simply could not make a major change in my life based on theory, even though the theory might be true. Looking back I knew real faith would result in real change, and I did not have real faith. For me at that time I knew something else needed to happen. Of course God knew this, and something did happen. I have to say it was by no means immediate, and God seems to want to make us wait longer than we would choose. For me the misery lasted well over a year.

In February 1975 the Christian Union at Nottingham University had organised a mission, and a man called David Watson had come to speak. He was a Church of England vicar, and had become well-known as a gifted speaker. More than that, he spoke a great deal about

Five loaves and two fishes

the Holy Spirit, encouraging his hearers to re-discover the Spirit's presence and transforming power.

On this night I stood outside the meeting, smoking, wondering whether to cross the threshold. Eventually I did, but only by one metre. The meeting was in full swing, with David Watson speaking in his winsome, compelling way. He spoke of Jesus, the man, the author of life, the miracle worker, and the one who wanted to meet and know me. His portrayal of Jesus struck a chord. Many years later I read what C S Lewis wrote, "when we meet him, we shall know that we have always known him". And the Jesus that David Watson spoke of was someone my deepest heart seemed already to recognise. There was an inner connection. An encounter. I realised this incredible Jesus was worth all I possessed, all I had or might ever achieve, and all I hoped for.

I heard David Watson calling people forward to meet Jesus, and to start a walk with him. The whole process from crossing the threshold into the meeting, to stumbling to the front, took me no more than 30 minutes. But as I knelt at the front, and David Watson laid his hands on me and prayed for me, my life would never be the same. I often say my life pivoted around that moment in time.

Five loaves and two fishes

Myra had already responded, and now for us both there began a real journey of faith. It was very apparent to the people around us that something very powerful had occurred, and over the following months we influenced many to respond to Jesus. We became committed followers and were greatly helped by both the structured discipling training of the Navigators, and also by the wonderful charismatic pastoring of David Huggett, then vicar of St Nicolas's church, Nottingham.

The Navigators ingrained within us a desire to "Go into all the world and make disciples" from Jesus clear and last command. Their motto was "to know Christ and make him known". We remain deeply grateful for the grounding the Navigators gave us. Around that time, Ron and Bette Finlay took the lead in the Nottingham Navigators, and they demonstrated a wonderful mix of giving us a long leash, but also keeping us accountable. Though Bette has gone to be with the Lord, Ron remains a good friend.

We were married in 1976 and the call to mission came soon after in the shape of Isaiah 58:6-12;
> *6"Is not this the kind of fasting I have chosen: to loose the chains of injustice and untie the cords of the yoke, to set the oppressed free and break every yoke?*

Five loaves and two fishes

Is it not to share your food with the hungry and to provide the poor wanderer with shelter - when you see the naked, to clothe him, and not to turn away from your own flesh and blood?

8 Then your light will break forth like the dawn, and your healing will quickly appear; then your righteousness will go before you, and the glory of the LORD will be your rear guard.

9 Then you will call, and the LORD will answer; you will cry for help, and he will say: Here am I. "If you do away with the yoke of oppression, with the pointing finger and malicious talk, 10 and if you spend yourselves in behalf of the hungry and satisfy the needs of the oppressed, then your light will rise in the darkness, and your night will become like the noonday.

11 The LORD will guide you always; he will satisfy your needs in a sun-scorched land and will strengthen your frame. You will be like a well-watered garden,

like a spring whose waters never fail.

12 Your people will rebuild the ancient ruins and will raise up the age-old foundations; you will be called Repairer of Broken Walls, Restorer of Streets with Dwellings.

Five loaves and two fishes

What turned out to be a key event occurred in 1977. The Navigators asked us to attend a European disciple-making congress - the ECDM which stood for the European Congress for Disciple-making. It was in Essen, Germany. I remember the good coffee which was so rare in the UK at that time. And the fact that virtually every one of the 3,000 people there spoke English. But the enduring memory was of Myra and I standing up together, holding hands and responding to the challenge: 'Who will go wherever God sends?' We had been married 6 months and it was to be another year before we would qualify as doctors. We were convinced that, from that point on, our medical degrees would be kingdom passports to get us into places and situations that would otherwise be difficult. We came back home determined to invest our spiritual, emotional, financial and professional lives in his kingdom. I look back on this and it was enormously important. Many folk today ask how they could be more committed. The fact is commitment is a decision, where we draw a line in the sand.

We had a testing time a few months later, as we went to Pakistan for our 'elective'. This is a period of time abroad to consolidate medical training. Six weeks in a rural desert mission hospital should have put us off, but it didn't. We celebrated our first wedding anniversary with a curry from the local bazaar. It turned out so hot we could not eat it. We tentatively

Five loaves and two fishes

left it out for the local hospital dog, fearing for his welfare. In order to extinguish his tongue we left some water for him, but he gobbled the food happily, wagged his tail and wandered off. He ignored the water, apparently content to have been invited to the English missionaries first wedding anniversary.

During that time we learned a little of Islam from the inside, and the realities of what could, and could not be achieved in long term mission. For us it was foundational. We realised that for white, western, Christian people to hope to connect with these tribal people was a massive step. Some made a connection like our American friend Bob. He had been in Karachi for decades. Though he was American, he had learned Urdu and spoke it like a local. Every day his job (as far as I could determine) was to get on buses and sell gospel tracts to the locals. These days in Pakistan he would be imprisoned on day one and subjected to an unknown fate soon after. His wife was called Ruth, and she taught the poor children of whom there were many due to untreated trachoma. Trachoma is a chlamydial infection of the eye, affecting millions even today, and resulting in blindness in at least one million as I write. Many are children. Treatment at an early stage is completely curative and costs about 30p. Our charity, New Hope (www.newhope.co.uk) has treated thousands.

Five loaves and two fishes

They were not short-term missionaries. They had gone for life. Both are now with the Lord, and we stand in awe of their example.

Having a good scriptural foundation, then being filled with the Holy Spirit, I was occupied in my thinking at this time about the power of God. In particular, why was it so little in evidence? After all, scripture is bold in its promise:
> *His divine power has given us everything we need for life and godliness through our knowledge of him who called us by his own glory and goodness. (2 Peter 1:3)*

I reasoned that if we have the Holy Spirit, whom is not given in measure (ie not rationed[xiii]), why should we be so bereft of his power? This was not consistent with all I read in the New Testament. Slowly I worked out the divine equation, described so concisely by Mike Breen[xiv]. Physicists know that current (ie power = P) is the result of voltage (V) divided by resistance (R). The voltage from heaven is high, and unchanging. The part that varies is our resistance. If it is high the maths is plain: the power in our lives is low. If we can lower our resistance to all God has for us, the power begins to flow.

Now that's all great in theory. But the rubber hits the road when we consider something we might be

Five loaves and two fishes

resistant to. It may be the need to alter our career path, give away some money, offer our valuable time to benefit someone else, bring a relationship fully under his direction or be open to the gifts and ministry of the Holy Spirit. So I did all I could to yield to God. A daily prayer at that time was written on the first page of my journal, words taken from a hymn by Frederick Brookes:

> *My goal is God Himself, not joy, nor peace,*
> *Nor even blessing, but Himself, my God;*
> *'Tis His to lead me there—not mine, but His—*
> *At any cost, dear Lord, by any road.*

In Nottingham there is a park known as Woodthorpe Park. It is quite high, giving great views of a large sector of the city and its' surroundings. I was discipling a friend at that time, and the two of us would meet at 5am and pray over the city for two hours. I look back with the perspective of years, and feel I might have been better to have had coffee with my neighbours and to commit to pray for them and their concerns for 30 minutes a day. But God sees our earnestness.

My earnestness also took the form of going into the local Nottingham pubs to "witness" to the unwitting. Mostly people told us to get lost, but one day we met Andy in "The Plainsman". Amazingly he recognised my friend Chris from the hospital we worked in, and

Five loaves and two fishes

the two had already engaged in some conversation about the gospel. But that night he was ready to respond. We led him to Jesus then and there. I fixed to have a quiet time with him the next day and discovered his office was very close to mine. Andy was a man of the world, and the challenges of discipling him were significant. But he was great fun and he soon became part of our growing 'Medics ministry'. Others joined us and we enjoyed our times together, laying on lightweight evangelistic events for friends and neighbours. We did not know, but we were exploring missional community, and many of those involved grew and multiplied. Our little medics group grew to over a dozen, many finding Christ for the first time. We are in touch with most to this day. We met up with Andy recently and it was a tremendous joy to see how his life has unfolded, and how he has touched many others' lives.

No longer were we reluctant disciples. We had seen something of the kingdom in the community through changed lives. We had tasted something very special and we were now committed to getting more, and taking others with us. Our time in Pakistan was formative and we imagined this would propel us into a life of ministry overseas.

Five loaves and two fishes

Chapter 2 - Passports please - John

We qualified in 1978 and had to apply for our mandatory 120 hour per week 'house jobs' which lasted one year. The year was broken into two 6 month jobs, one in medicine and one in surgery.

We were reasonable students but not the best and there was great competition for teaching hospital jobs. As I hoped to pursue a surgical career it was imperative that one of our house jobs was in a teaching hospital. As the hours were so horrendous we both needed to get jobs together or we would never have seen one another. It seemed a tall order when we had so many talented colleagues.

As we prayed about the situation Myra was drawn to verses in Numbers 14 when the Israelites sent spies to investigate the promised land and they came back terrified declaring that there were "giants in the land". Two of the spies, however, were not perturbed. They said "Yes there are giants but GOD IS WITH US." We claimed this promise for the jobs we needed and we got them!

So we started at Nottingham City Hospital in August 1978. It was quite intimidating as so much responsibility rested on the 'house man'. The week was made up of normal 8 hour days, with an

Five loaves and two fishes

alternating 24 hours on call, becoming 72 hours every other weekend. It was gruelling and not to be recommended, but our medics group used to meet, pray and support one another. Most members of this group, now near to retirement, remember the fellowship and community fondly.

The on call was made doubly challenging by the fact that Dr Sloan and Dr Sloan shared a bed, so the phone rang regularly through most nights. It was a great time of learning, but we were glad to complete it. Shortly before this time, my Dad had passed away, and we felt a commitment to care for my Mum, now alone. This rather upset our initial thinking that we would move overseas in the period after qualifying, but we felt God had his plan.

I started studying for the "Primary FRCS", a formidable exam that had a low pass rate. Overall it was around 30%, but most passed on their second, third (or more) attempts. It was rumoured that the fist time pass rate was 5%. To prepare for the exam I spent a year teaching at my old medical school. As I was teaching the subjects that the exam comprised, it was good preparation. When the time for the exam came, several of us went up to Edinburgh to take it. The day before I had been reading Revelation 3, and the writings to the Church in Philadelphia. As I read verse 8 God spoke to me *"I know your works. Look! I have*

Five loaves and two fishes

put in front of you an open door that no one can shut. You have only a little strength, but you have kept my word and have not denied my name". I knew God was telling me the open door was that I would pass the exam. I was so excited as I knew this for a certainty. Then I also knew that I must tell my friends before the exam, so they might believe in the Living God! So I found some words to tell them. At that time they just thought I was off my head, but when my pass was announced, several began to show interest.

Soon after, we were asked to think about attending a Navigator Medics meeting in Bergen, Norway. It was about making disciples in a medical context. This was a tremendous opportunity to consider other ways forward, as we had a strong disciple-making desire, and wanted to discover how it could work in our circles in UK medicine. It seemed as if God was about to open a new door.

We set off from our home in Nottingham and drove the 2 hour journey to Newcastle airport. We still felt like lovebirds, and our first child was on his way. Going abroad was exciting. At the airport we parked our battered car in the car park among much nicer models, and made our way to the check in.

We found the check-in desk easily. "Passports please" said the official. We looked at each other with

Five loaves and two fishes

increasing horror. Passports! Of course. We needed to have them. But they were two hours away, tucked away in a drawer at home. We explained in earnest that we needed to get to a conference in Bergen, but that we had forgotten our passports. The check in official reflected, then said, "Well, it is not essential for me, and I can let you go through, but I don't think passport control will take the same view".

That was good enough for us, so we moved on. At passport control the official held out his hand for our passports. "We have forgotten them" we confessed nervously. All the time we were praying. Border control was tight and it was not to relax for another two decades. Norway was not (and is still not) in the European Union, and the open borders of Schengen did not include Norway until 2001.

The official said we could sign a form to leave the UK, but would not be able to enter Norway. That was good enough for us. After all, the most important step you ever take is the next one.

So we boarded the plane and, in due course, landed in Bergen. The conversation was becoming routine. "Passports please" said the official in perfect English. "We have forgotten them" we said in our best confessional tone. "How did you get here?" he said, amazed. We told him what had happened and

Five loaves and two fishes

showed him the copy of the paper we had signed. "Why have you come to Norway?" he asked. We explained about the Christian Medical conference and how important it was to us. Incredibly, he let us through. "But you won't be able to leave the country easily" he said.

The conference was great. We made some friends and sharpened our focus. Our medicine clearly was to be a passport for us. Maybe God was humouring us in this, proving that it would get us beyond borders, even without ordinary passports.

Suffice to say that the journey home was the same in reverse. The whole thing was a series of miracles that still amazes us today, over 35 years later. It was the first time we knew for sure we were serving a King, and under his protection.

Soon after our first child, Tim was born. I still remember the incredible sense of a heart bursting with love and joy, plus elation, pride, responsibility and gratitude. Our lives were never to be the same again. We had a little person whom we loved and who depended on us.

Myra was starting her training as a general practitioner (family doctor). She took baby Tim with her, fed him between patients, and amazingly got on with life. I

Five loaves and two fishes

realised I had married an absolute star! Meanwhile I pursued my surgical training. It was so good to dip into so many aspects of surgery, and I loved the experience it brought. It was not possible to sit the "FRCS" surgical exam until 4 years from qualification, but as soon as I could, I went for it.

I used to get up at 5am to pray then do 2 hours study while my mind was fresh. That way I was able to spend time with Myra and Tim in the evenings. I passed the FRCS just as Becci was born. Poor Myra was juggling two little ones, 16 months apart, with a husband who was still working 80 plus hours each week and every third night on call.

More than that, I was preaching regularly around churches in Nottingham. I look back and wonder what kingdom effect I had, but I was earnest and God knew my heart. And I was offering my loaves and fishes as best I could.

Life as a believer contains heartaches as well as joys. Today I feel so sad to hear some preachers describe a fantasy life of success and prosperity that can be yours. The reality is that we will know difficulty and suffering without a doubt. The truth is that He walks with us through all life brings. One of the men I had led to Jesus was also my best friend. He was a doctor and was on duty the night Tim was born, soon after we

Five loaves and two fishes

returned from Norway. I learned an important lesson that helping someone become a disciple was easier than helping them mature into someone who could make disciples. Over a period of years we prayed together, did bible study and spent a lot of fun time in each other's company. When he married, I was privileged to be his best man. As time passed he became troubled and sought help for depression. We spent many hours together, but I felt powerless to help. At that stage I really knew nothing about praying for people in power. I had a view of healing that it had all stopped in the first century.

I was on a medical attachment in Chicago, USA when I got a call from Myra. My dear friend had taken his own life. He had written two notes. One for his wife and one for me. I was devastated. I flew back for his funeral with a leaden heart, lots of questions and many tears.

But the whole experience had a fundamental effect on me. I suddenly knew I needed to learn to see sick people made well, and I determined to find out how to minister like Jesus. Life's events overtake however, and good intentions don't generally deliver all we wish for. So nothing happened on the healing front for a while. It turned out to be God's timing.

Five loaves and two fishes

Around this time we saw our gorgeous daughter Becci born, and a couple of years later our third baby, another son whom we named James. Life was full and our little family was an absolute joy. We look back and wonder how we found the time and energy to raise three children, work in demanding medical roles, and remain actively involved in our church and medics group.

Some years passed, and in 1987, we moved to Leeds where I started a consultant job. My senior colleague was Michael Flowers, who was a believer and a godly man. He rapidly became my mentor. The church he helped lead was in a mini-revival. Unbelievers would visit and sense the presence of God.

Initially we stayed in hospital accommodation, which was of very poor stock. Baby James was in a cot in a moderately sized room with a roof light above. One weekend we went to visit family and moved his cot to a side wall. When we returned on the Sunday night there had been a storm and the roof light had fallen into the room. A large piece of glass, 30 cm long was protruding vertically, impaled in the floor. It had been exactly where the cot usually was, and certainly would have killed James. Once again, Father was looking after us.

Five loaves and two fishes

That year we became aware of the teachings of John Wimber, who was a charismatic church pastor from California. He was determined to see new testament miracles happen. This struck a chord from a few years before, and we attended a number of his conferences. We learned a great deal, but perhaps the most significant was to experience God's presence in worship. This led to learning to pray for the sick. We saw a miraculous healing right in front of our eyes. Someone with a large goitre (swelling of the thyroid) was being prayed for in the row behind us. We saw it shrink to normal size over a few seconds. We might be many things, but being gullible in the area of physical healing is not on our list. This was a class A healing! A new phase began as we moved into an amazing walk, using spiritual gifts in a way that we had longed for.

The phrase "Spiritual Gifts" evokes many different reactions in the hearts of believers. Some have embraced it for a long time. Some are new to such things. Some are suspicious. I can understand why. From time to time people have behaved so strangely in this area, scriptural truth has been scarce, and wild claims have been made. But Jesus didn't say we needed to be weird. Essentially he said the church started with the release of the Holy Spirit, its growth was to be fuelled by the same Holy Spirit, and everyone would find their place and role through the

Five loaves and two fishes

Holy Spirit. So its fairly straightforward. We need to embrace the Holy Spirit, all the time staying normal!

So we soon prayed for everyone we could. We knew that all healings that were claimed, need to be evaluated. We have seen some claims that, as medics, were embarrassing. Some of these had simply not occurred, and it devalued the kingdom to claim otherwise. "Leg lengthening" is one such claim. A shorter leg is almost always due to an abnormal tilt of the pelvis. Relax the muscles around the pelvis and the short leg "grows". It may be wise to discuss with someone more expert when you believe you have seen a healing to avoid this kind of embarrassment. Meanwhile some healings have occurred, but are 'class B' ie the person may have got better anyway (such as praying for someone with a headache). That's not a bad thing, especially if you are the one with the headache. But class A healings cannot occur spontaneously by the rules we know. They include a cancer going away, HIV status going from positive to negative, or a progressive disease being reversed and resolving.

A young Turkish man came to live near us, and we quickly befriended him. He was a Muslim. One day he injured his ankle and a good friend of ours prayed that it would be healed. Apparently it was healed immediately, and Mohammed (name changed for

Five loaves and two fishes

security) accepted Jesus the same day. He moved in with us and we sought to teach him all we knew. He lived with us for a year, becoming a trusted family member, much loved by our three children. The immersion in family life provided a powerful means of discipling him, and in fact, I don't think there would have been any other way. We are still in contact with each other, three decades later.

Our conversations at mealtimes were interesting. He told us one day that he hated the Jews, a fairly standard Muslim view. Myra endeavoured to explain this was a little tricky as the Jesus he was choosing to follow was one of them! He was unconvinced, but God resolved the problem a few weeks later when he was locked out one night. He said he would not be home and we had dead-bolted the front door. He tried to sleep in the garden but got very cold, even though it was summer. One of the problems with hypothermia is that fits can be induced in some people. As Mohammed got fed up in the garden, in the early hours he wandered down to the local shops where he collapsed and had a fit outside the local Jewish bakery, which was preparing bagels for the morning. The kindly old baker called the ambulance and stayed with him until it arrived. The two became good friends! God has a wonderful way of reversing our prejudices as he gradually changes us!

Five loaves and two fishes

It was now over 10 years since we had qualified. I had trained as a surgeon as I felt this would be most useful outside the UK. Myra trained as a GP so that our skills complemented. At that time I was a deacon in the local Baptist Church. The mini revival was still going on in that church, and the sense of God's glory was like a mist in the evening service. One day the youth worker encountered a scruffy 17 year old wanting prayer. The youth pastor wanted another person to pray with him. I think it must have been the youth's first time in church, and he had just come under conviction. His name was David. While we prayed with him he confessed that he had broken into the local school the day before and "removed" a number of 'BBC' computers. These were the state-of-the-art computers at that time. He wanted to put things right. As we prayed, I saw him as if in the future, wearing a suit and looking smart and educated. It was as if God was telling us to have confidence that the Holy Spirit would truly transform him. We prayed, and the next morning I called the head of the school. The agreement was that all the computers would be returned and the damage paid for. If so, the police would not press charges, which is exactly what happened.

Following this, David lived with us for a period and the promised transformation enfolded in front of our eyes. Some years later he gained a degree, married a

Five loaves and two fishes

doctor and started a career in the local University. He is now an established University Lecturer, a father and youth leader in his local church. How we need God's insights.

By 1990 we were ready for the next stage of mission - planting a church.

Five loaves and two fishes

Chapter 3 - Church planting to medical mission - John

Michael and June mentored us in a very natural way. Their gentle manner allowed us to trust them. In doing so, we absorbed their Holy Spirit perspectives.

I had been exposed to a lot of mentoring by this stage. I liked the idea but not the experience. But now my key question was answered. I had always struggled with experiences of being discipled or mentored by a peer. I am sure it was part pride. But it was also part reality.

Whilst one can challenge another, that is mutual encouragement, not mentoring. I could not see that a young adult could really help another young adult in a significant way. That is suggesting that one person gets a lot of wisdom and revelation, while another remains in the dark. I knew enough by the age of 30 to appreciate this was unlikely.

But Michael had 5 grown children and over 20 years experience beyond me. He had worked in Bangladesh and Nepal. Most of all he followed and loved God. And I trusted him. As a result, each morning I arrived early at work and we prayed for all our staff by name. At lunchtime we would talk about revival. He opened familiar scriptures in unfamiliar ways. In the space of weeks I learned more than I had done in years.

Five loaves and two fishes

Michael and June were running "Kinship Groups" which were like an extended family. They were missional communities in all but name! We reached out to unbelievers and saw many come to Christ. We reached up to God in Spirit-led prayer and worship. We sought revelation, and ministered to each other. Most of all, we held each other in high esteem, being committed to each other as new testament family.

In 1989 after doing several locum jobs Myra was offered a post in Chapeltown Health Centre, which resonated with all her desires to work amongst the poor and needy. The building was in an inner city area of Leeds and in the red light district.

Patients came from all ethnic backgrounds and so it was a very colourful place to work. Its darker history was that this was the place where the Yorkshire Ripper had abducted and murdered most of his victims.

In her first few weeks she had to deal with a very stroppy young black woman who clearly thought that the new doctor was a stuck up snob who needed to be challenged. So the early consultations were a little rocky but a basis of trust and respect was eventually established to such an extent that in due course, Blossom would see no other doctor. Her house was a mid terrace in a run down street and stood out because of the brand new windows with grills, and the

Five loaves and two fishes

wrought iron gate over the front door. People suspected that there was some drug related activity in the home.

One day Blossom came into the surgery in great distress because the police had cut open her front door with an oxyacetylene torch and arrested her son. This seemed to have triggered a deep depression and she was low and withdrawn in contrast to her previous ebullient self. During one consultation for her depression, Myra asked if she had any support connections with the local church to which she responded "They wouldn't have me 'cos I've always walked on the wild side" she said. A discussion ensued around the unconditional love of Jesus but went no further. Many months later, just before we moved away from Leeds, Blossom came in looking total different in her disposition. It transpired that she had gone to the local black Pentecostal church and met Jesus. She was transformed! Having left her old ways behind she was applying to train as a nurse. After 15 years of knowing her it was a joy for Myra to see the transformation.

Myra's years in Chapeltown were very formative. Her patient mix was roughly 40% of Asian origin, 30% Caribbean and the remainder made out of many other ethnic minorities and a few white British or Irish. She really enjoyed getting to know the families and watching babies grow towards adulthood. She

Five loaves and two fishes

appreciated the privilege of sharing sorrows and joys with patients over the many years of close relationship that was the domain of a family doctor in that era. She had several long letters from patients revealing secrets they had harboured for decades.

There were many funny episodes as well as sad ones. There were times when she was very aware of the angels keeping her safe in some hairy situations usually related to psychiatric patients. Two of her patients were murdered during her time in the area and several others died of drug overdose. The local pub was an infamous drug den but one spring she had to do several postnatal visits to a woman with a baby who was living on the premises. Happily the customers in the bar directed her to the flat and didn't offer her any drugs!

The reception staff were a mine of invaluable information and often warned her about this one or that one and especially the guy who seemed remarkably nice but had done time for murder. When a visit came through for a child with asthma it was so helpful to be told that the child's father had died in an acute asthma attack or to know that the husband of a depressed woman had shot himself in the garden shed. The Jamaican receptionist who was into her fifties had been a bareback elephant rider with the circus in a previous life. She was great asset in a busy evening

Five loaves and two fishes

surgery because she knew all the local West Indian lads from childhood and tolerated no nonsense from anyone trying to squeeze into an already overbooked surgery.

When she had been given the job in Chapeltown she really felt God had put her there and believed he would use her to change lives in Chapeltown. After several years she realised that God had put her there so Chapeltown would change her life.

As the months passed, we realised we worked well with Michael and June and could form a great team. We began to dream dreams. Within a year we really wanted to get going. Church planting was the modus operandi of the day. If you were serious about kingdom growth you planted a church. New Wine was brimming with it. And so were we. And as we prayed for a suitable location, I had a prophetic picture of part of a building. The problem was all I saw was the floor! We didn't know where it was. But it was a nice parquet floor and we presumed it was where we needed our church plant to be. I thought the picture looked like a school or a dance floor. We had already tried the schools and there were no openings. But there was one dance studio nearby, called Street Lane Studio. When we approached the proprietor, called Edna, she was amazingly receptive.

Five loaves and two fishes

So on the first Sunday of April 1990 we gathered 50 people and started a new fellowship - part of our Baptist Church. It was on Street Lane, so we called it Street Lane Fellowship. The name still evokes passion in a few ageing hearts! God blessed our passion. Prophets emerged, children grew, and new believers were added. We served doughnuts at half time. Corinne Bailey-Rae grew up there. We prayed unashamedly for the needy. And when J John, the famous evangelist visited, we felt we were credible! Michael mentored me in preaching, giving lots of opportunity and encouragement, but correction when I got it wrong.

In 1992 we signed up for the first Alpha training course at Holy Trinity Brompton Church in London. The Alpha course helps relatively unchurched people to grasp the gospel of Jesus and respond to it. Nicky Gumbel had begun to develop this in 1990, and it grew rapidly from just 4 courses in 1991 to 2,500 in 1995. By1998, 10,500 courses were run. In 2015, the Alpha website described it as running in 169 countries, in 112 languages, with over 27 million people having been involved.

So we started Alpha courses. One wonderful disciple was Kerry (name changed for privacy). We realised that Kerry was an angry woman when she joined our first course. Myra was leading a small discussion

Five loaves and two fishes

group and she turned on her with eyes blazing to demand why God is "Father" and not "Mother". As we got to know her better we became aware of the terrible and damaging relationship she had experienced with her father. This had been so bad that she had changed her surname.

Her paternal experience clouded all her subsequent male relationships and she had left the father of her child before the birth took place. All her more recent relationships had been with women. One day she asked to meet with us both. We knew why she wanted to meet. So she asked us about her orientation and whether Jesus could accept her. Christians get bad press over their perceived difficulty in accepting gay issues, but I believe as Jesus never mentioned it he wanted to put this aside and simply accept and love all people. So I told her that she needed to park the matter as unimportant to Jesus, and simply learn to love Him. I told her that he would whisper his thoughts to her, and all would be clearer in due course. So it was quite amazing that she was able to begin to put her trust in this man called Jesus as she grew in her understanding of him.

Although her background had been difficult she loved Jesus from the start. In fact, like in the parable, she sold everything to gain the pearl of knowing him. We had never seen a new believer take off like that. She

Five loaves and two fishes

proved Mike Breen's power theory that as our resistance to God drops, the power in our lives increases. She certainly offered her new Jesus no resistance, and so her life became full of his power. As a result her life deeply affected many others. When she asked Myra to hear her confession of all her sexual sin it was a deeply humbling experience.

Kerry had been a dance teacher and began to turn her skills to dancing in worship. This was indescribably powerful. She travelled to South Africa to take part in a large international dance conference. Her love for Jesus was infectious and she told everyone about the phenomenal difference he had made to her life.

After some months she felt led to contact the father of her child and her 8 year-old son was introduced to the father he had never known. He was able to develop a strong bond despite the lost years and they spent time together regularly.

Suddenly, she became ill, and the diagnosis was of cancer. She was so young! And yet from the outset we suspected that Jesus might want her as his prize. We watched as the disease took hold. Slowly she began to fade away. Of course we were all desperate for a divine healing, and we fasted and prayed for her. But as the days passed, God's intentions filtered through to us, as we all (Kerry included) understood

Five loaves and two fishes

that truly, Jesus was calling her home. Healing was not to be. When she died, so many turned up for the funeral. My friend Joe and I led the service, though it was really a tearful celebration. The place was packed! People were standing in the doorways. We wondered if she had spoken about her Jesus to everyone in North Leeds!

By the mid 1990's we were seeking God's leading for the future, and that summer were visiting Nîmes, a beautiful compact Roman city 30km away from France's Mediterranean coast. Over the course of the previous 6 years we had built up a friendship with a French family who lived there, and we had exchanged children on an annual basis. As a result, our families had become good friends. And remain so.

Towards the end of a Sunday service at their Assemblies of God church, an elderly lady started to pray for us, and quickly moved into prophecy. She was called Madeline, was probably 80 years old, and she was known to regularly pray with prophetic accuracy. She said God was going to give us a new hope, and she saw signposts, which read "obey". She described us being in a river, which was only up to our ankles. As we obeyed we went deeper and found the water was up to our hips. As we obeyed it went deeper up to our shoulders. And after that our feet

Five loaves and two fishes

could no longer touch the bottom and we had to swim, moved by the flowing current.

It was a picture from Ezekiel 47 of letting go of human control, and trusting him. The sense was of the future, characterised by this. As with many such words, we recorded them, discussed them between ourselves, shared them with trusted friends and prayed over them. We did not try to consciously work this out, nor did we discuss it widely with others.

About 2 years later we began to move into a model of church known as "Cell Church" which offers a healthy mix of small cell and large celebration, and felt an increasing burden to reach the needy. We were not sure church was doing a great job being good news to those who most needed to hear it. People like Lawrence Singlehurst from Youth with a Mission (YWAM) came to advise us, and we were near to Howard Astin in Bradford who had applied cell church principles in a Church of England context. We pulled a team together and took some time away to pray and plan. One thing we needed was a new name, one which captured our purpose. We stood back from this as we wanted some real ownership from the team. In a time of prayer and prophecy the team felt God was raising the name "New Hope" within their hearts. With amazement we called the new work "New Hope" inwardly realising Madeline

Five loaves and two fishes

had prophesied about this a couple of years before. This understandably confirmed to us we were on the right path.

One of our number led a lady called Jenny (named changed) to Jesus. Her life was in a mess. I don't mean the sort of mess we often see. This was beyond our comprehension. Jenny's 15-year-old daughter had just been murdered, and the father of the murderer was Jenny's live-in partner. The murderer was her stepson. He went to jail. Her partner was distraught beyond measure. Soon after he took his own life. The tragedy was profound, and Jenny was utterly crushed.

They lived on the notorious Gipton housing estate, which was said to be one of the biggest deprivation areas in Europe at that time. We felt as if we might be out of our depth. So we partnered with other churches to fund a Kidz Club, influenced by the American Bill Wilson, who had successfully established one in Liverpool with Frontline Church. His strap line was so good. "If you want to see God do something you haven't seen him do before, you are going to have to do something you've never done before".

So Becci (at this stage 15) and Myra would get on an empty bus every Saturday, and fill it with these love-deprived kids. The children would have a ball as, along with 300 others, they gathered for a great time of

Five loaves and two fishes

fun and kingdom good news. Myra and Becci would faithfully care for 100, and visit each and every one in their homes during the week. It was a powerful mix of love and meaningful relationship.

Madeline's prophecy had been spot on. We had a new hope, which by this time had become a registered charity. We had obeyed. And we were definitely immersed in water so deep our toes could no longer touch the bottom.

We started to work with Connections, a missional church network founded by Philip Mohabir. Philip was a servant leader and meeting him made us realise how unusual servant leaders were. Our good friend Michael was the same. Both were genuinely willing to lay their own lives down to see God's purpose fulfilled in others. We had come across a few church leaders who seemed unable to do this. The contrast was stark, and we determined which we would always seek to be.

Connections was all about relationship, and worked by networking pastors throughout the world. Philip asked us to consider developing medical missions. A start had been made by Drs Hugh Alberti and Dr Peter Heywood both from Middlesborough. So in 1999 I travelled with Peter to Guyana, South America, taking our eldest son Tim with us. By now he was 18 years

Five loaves and two fishes

old, on his gap year and had a place at medical school for the following year.

I recall the culture shock. There were no lights where we stayed, and no running water. As we arrived late at night, with a 5-hour clock rewind to cope with, we were too tired to care much. The morning brought tropical rain (which soaks you in a micro second), visions of lush, dense undergrowth and smells of Caribbean food, all of which were beyond our experience. We set off to an area known as the Pomeroon. Crossed by rivers and creeks, road navigation was impossible (the word Guyana means land of many rivers) and we took to flimsy, but fast boats. We arrived quite late in an Amerindian village and we were given an old mattress to sleep on, without sheets. We were in a covered hut with open sides. The next morning Tim and I woke and we counted the tarantulas sitting inside the roof, looking down on us. I think there were 17, or maybe 19. No matter, there were considerably more than were welcome. These creatures spanned around 15cm and they could move faster than human eyes could follow. We left them to their own devices.

The same day we started the clinic. "It's a bush clinic", Peter explained. "You pick a bush to give you some shade and then you start". More than a hundred of these lovely indigenous Amerindians turned up and

Five loaves and two fishes

we listened to their chests, treated their malaria and advised on their babies. They spoke a sort of English, but heavily accented. And they used strange terms, like "eye swing" (dizziness) and they said things like "when me need to drink de tablets doc?"

Coffee time came and I was offered "sky juice". I wondered if Rupert Murdoch had got here first, though I doubted it. My philosophy has always been to say yes to any local offering, so I watched as a young chap scrambled up a fairly tall coconut tree, harvest a couple of coconuts, and present them to us. With a single machete blow, the top came off, and there was the sky juice inside. Very welcome!

The key man was Pastor Yasin, known as the "apostle to the interior". He had planted several dozen churches along the Essequibo river, mostly among the indigenous Amerindian people. He lived at Bartica, which might mean "the end of civilisation as you know it" but I can't be sure of that. The Essequibo is near, and similar to the Amazon. It is 20km wide in places, hosts crocodiles and piraña, and has lots of submerged rocks. As a consequence, people don't do well if their boats capsize, and capsizing is not rare.

Pastor Yasin, as the astute reader will know from the name, started life as a Muslim. He tells the story of becoming a driver in his free time, while training as an

Five loaves and two fishes

Imam. He was asked by his high school teacher, a Christian, to drive him to an evangelistic convention. He did, but stayed outside, feeling aversion to the proceedings. He had great respect for the teacher who was affected by paralysis. That very night, his teacher was healed. Jesus had apparently done this. Despite the inevitable rejection and family persecution, through this event Yasin subsequently accepted Christ. Like many Muslim converts to Christ, he was not casual in his faith. He is one of the most determined and effective pastors and evangelists I know. Often following a clinic, we would share the gospel. He would say to me "Don't tell them too much about love, remember to tell them they are going to hell. They can find out about the love later!"

It took 8 hours by boat to go south to the village of Micobi. About 300 indigenous Amerindians live there, and a delightful lady called Princess ran the church. We would hold a clinic all day and preach by kerosene hurricane lamps at night.

In this environment I learned to preach "ad lib", with zero notice, often re-telling a parable and explaining it in terms of the villager's worldview. I had been preaching for 20 years at this stage, but this was new. Pastor Yasin would wrap up my preach and we would pray for new believers, then baptise them at dawn.

Five loaves and two fishes

Yasin was full of faith and his stories were designed to help others trust God more fully. He recounted to us how he had been preaching after dark by the light of a kerosene lamp on a table under a coconut tree. At the end of his message, a large snake dropped from the tree above and broke the lamp plunging everything into darkness. The assembled faithful suddenly saw heaven (or hell) a great deal closer and ran in every direction!

Tropical days start and end abruptly around 6am and 6pm. By 7am it is often over 30 degrees centigrade in Guyana. The abundance of rivers results in a very high humidity. If you have not experienced this, it means you perspire so heavily by 8am you need to have a change of clothes. It's not just the heat and light that wake you. It's the animals too. The cockerels really ought to connect to atomic clocks as they start to predict dawn 3 hours too early. But worse than that is the "dog tennis". That starts around the same time. Dogs in Guyana aren't often pedigrees. Usually they are brown, short haired creatures whose DNA has been mixed up from every known breed. They vary fractionally in terms of size and aggression, but mostly they look alike. And they all love dog tennis. It starts with one dog serving a bark. Another, maybe half a kilometre away returns serve with a precise volley bark. The first barks the return to the back line and the lucky winner spins a final "ruff" over the net for a great

Five loaves and two fishes

drop-shot. And so it goes on. Often it's doubles. Sometimes it's Wimbledon and dozens play at once. Anyway, it's not great for sleeping.

So when Pastor Yasin comes at dawn I am awake. "Dr John, you are baptising the three who accepted Christ last night" he would say with delight. "When?" I reply. "Now" he would say, already going down to the river. At the muddy banks the boat captain was awake, complaining about the crocodiles who had been smacking the boat all night.

As I slowly got into the water I recalled Madeline's words. There were piranha and crocodiles in this water! There had been a 15 metre anaconda spotted locally. When I asked those being baptised if they would give their lives fully to Jesus, there was poignancy about it. It felt like a Christian "Jaws" remake. They always said yes with fervour, I prayed for them, immersed them and we all clambered out while we could.

Bathing was no easier. There was no running water, so the river was the bathroom. We gained confidence from the little children who skipped in and out of the water. None seemed to be missing any vital body parts.

Five loaves and two fishes

We visited Micobi, and similar villages, regularly. On one trip there we were caught out by leaving too late. So we pulled up to an isolated water pumping station as it was on concrete stilts and we could therefore string our hammocks up easily. There were five of us, and we had 4 hammocks. Someone was going to need to sleep on the ground. This was one of the worst decisions I had ever faced. I truly could not offer to sleep on the ground where snakes, tarantulas and poisonous caterpillars roamed. Nor could any of the team. No matter, Pastor Yasin, easily 10 years older than me, and true servant, stretched out on a piece of cardboard and was asleep before any of us.

We had to wrap mosquito nets around our hammocks. This is not easy, and there should be an Olympic class for this aspect of gymnastics. The coup de grace was getting out in the night to visit the "bathroom". As if this were not difficult enough, once achieved, a further challenge existed. There were eyes looking at us as we shone our torches and the eyes winked back. We learned these were the eyes of jaguars, quietly observing us. Meanwhile Yasin slept on like a baby.

Around Easter 2000 we took the whole family with us. Tim now 19, and ready for his medical training, was very useful in the clinics. I often watched him and wondered whether he really needed to go to medical school - he was a natural! Becci, who was 17 was

Five loaves and two fishes

wonderful with the children, teaching them to draw and paint. James was 14, and his mission was to teach these cricket-loving children the more wonderful game of football. We took 12 flat packed footballs begged from a Leeds sports shop.

The absolute remoteness of some of these places has to be seen. One man, Pastor Pooran, worked all week to support his family. At the weekend he would travel into the interior to a place known as "Great Falls". This would take many hours, involving wading through creeks waist deep. At this time we travelled with him. In order to get the whole family in boats we had to hire two. And so we set off. Beyond the point of no return we discovered the boat carrying the children had a serious leak, and it was getting worse. James was stalwartly bailing out the boat with a water bottle cut in half. I could see the boat gradually dropping in the water, and I could imagine the beasts below waiting for lunch! We made it to Great Falls just in time.

It was Easter Saturday, and I felt a bit of a fever developing. As evening came it got worse. I am not one to succumb readily to illness, so I passed it off and went to bed. The next morning I could not move. My temperature was above 40 degrees centigrade and I was ill. I was due to preach today! Yes, others could step in, but they wanted to hear the white visitor. They

Five loaves and two fishes

propped me up, leaning against a hut and I spoke. I am not sure how I managed. I was ill for days. It was not man flu, I was ill. When we got home I realised I had almost certainly contracted dengue fever. People think the mosquito only conveys malaria. But there is dengue fever, yellow fever and encephalitis too. Mosquitoes are the deadliest creatures on earth and malaria alone is one of the world's leading causes of death.

When we got home Philip Mohabir called me within 48 hours to ask how things had been. The leader of this global network called me! It seemed beyond reason. But such was his loving, servant heart.

By now we had no doubt Madeline's prophecy was right. How might we have reacted if we had understood all that this would mean from the safety of Nîmes 5 years earlier? And how might we have bypassed all God had for us if we had just gone overseas after qualifying? He has a plan for each of us, and no plan is the same as another. At this stage I recalled what J John had written in a book he gave me back in the Street Lane Fellowship days. He wrote "in His grip". And I knew we were.

Five loaves and two fishes

Chapter 4 - Learning to trust God on mission - John

We went to Guyana quite a lot. This was largely because of Philip Mohabir, as this had been his home.

Around this time he stayed in our home, and one morning he told me of a book he was writing. It was all about how the people of God were meant to be the instruments of his love and grace. I'd seen this characteristic first hand in Philip. With amazing humility he asked me what I thought he should name the book. "Hands of Jesus" I replied without much hesitation. After all, that's what we are. Sure enough, when the book was published, dear Philip had named it just that. He passed away in 2004, leaving an enormous gap and being sorely missed in the lives of many.

Guyana brought us many experiences, and many dear friends. We would arrive in Georgetown, jet lagged and weary, and go to Hauraruni, the Bible Training school late at night. Philip had started this years before in order to train pastors for the many churches he aimed to, and did, plant. I lost most of my culture shock visiting Pakistan and India many years earlier, but I was always surprised at the incredible tropical rain. No wonder everywhere was lush and green, and the land was criss-crossed by rivers.

Five loaves and two fishes

Haurauruni was really a clearing in the jungle, just a few degrees north of the equator. Faithful people keep it going, in adverse circumstances, so the kingdom can advance. Everywhere we went we met pastors who had been trained there. The vision and determination which lay behind this was impressive.

Many miles to the west, across the Demerara river, is Bartica. West, south and north is jungle, inhabited by Amerindian people in small settlements. Pastor Yasin has tirelessly worked with these people, and planted many churches. There is no robust communication network, nor a safe, rapid means of transport. Travel is by boat down the wide Essequibo river. In places it is narrow, the water boiling with turbulence as it passes over barely submerged rocks. Only experienced, licensed captains are legally permitted to navigate the river with passengers, and only by daylight.

At some stage around the year 2000, and I can't recall when, we met Deloris. She is shorter than me (and I am not tall), older than me, clearly Caribbean, and an absolute gem. So I call her my Mum. I say I am her albino son. Most people don't know how to respond! Deloris trained as a nurse, and over the years, learned to be a fiery preacher. And she was willing to go anywhere, and serve in any way necessary. That is the sort of team member you need!

Five loaves and two fishes

Deloris became a constant member of our team. We would travel for hours in an open motorboat to visit remote Amerindian villages.

In some villages we would encounter dogs, and their main purpose was to fend off unwelcome wildlife. However, in some villages we found none. When we asked Pastor Yasin why this might be, he simply replied "jaguars". It seemed that from time to time the jaguars would get the upper hand and carry the dogs away to feed on.

All this was quite amusing to the locals. During one open air clinic there was a commotion as a large snake had turned up. We wondered why our children, who were supposed to be running the pharmacy table, had disappeared. We found them in the clearing. A couple of Amerindian men had quickly found a chicken and a sac. We watched with fascination as we were taught how to catch a large snake in an open-air clinic! This was not a skill I expected to use much at home, but it seemed worth learning, all the same. The chicken is trapped at the bottom of the sac, and the sac placed near the snake. The snake realises there is a chicken on offer, and makes his way into the bag. Now for the skill. You close the bag, but this must not be too early or the snake might bite. And it can't be too late, or the snake will be making a rapid exit. But time it right and you catch the snake. So the

Five loaves and two fishes

mission was accomplished, we finished the clinic and all was well.

Sadly the capture and transport to market of these creatures is very lucrative for the villagers but not so good for the wildlife. Guyana is one of the last wilderness areas on earth due to its thick forest and difficult terrain. Some months before our visit the same villagers had caught a 30 foot anaconda and had a photo of a large number of them holding the poor creature before it was bagged up ready for the long boat trip to Georgetown. The following morning, however, the villagers had found an empty bag as the big snake had burst its way out and escaped to freedom.

On one occasion visiting Micobi, we arrived after dark in torrential rain. No sooner had we left our boat I was called to help a woman. Soaked through, I found some pieces of equipment and followed the guide. It was pitch black and we relied on my torch. I was taken into a circular, small grass hut. Inside there was light from a hurricane lamp. On a mat directly on the mud floor was a young woman, around 18 years old, in labour.

Now I have done a lot of different medical specialties in my training, but in obstetrics I had carried out ten normal deliveries as a medical student, and only one since.

Five loaves and two fishes

The situation was not good. Even I could determine that. She had been in labour around as many hours as she was old. I examined her and found a foetal heart beat, so I knew the baby was still alive. But her birth canal was less than 7cm wide, and I knew that 10cm was the key diameter. So I decided to use all my resources. All my tools and medicines in one go. I had one bite at the cherry. That translated into lots of pushing and lots of prayer. Beyond that my pockets were empty. We did this for 20 minutes. The rain hammered down. The poor girl looked exhausted.

It was late by now. Most villagers had gone to bed expecting to hear of a dead child, or a dead mother, or both in the morning. About 20 minutes later I put on my last pair of gloves to examine her. She was 10cm dilated. 'Fully' as they say in the trade. So I encouraged her to really push. Until then it was sort of token.

Around 40 minutes after I arrived in that simple grass hut, she delivered a baby boy. He was fine. Mum was fine. Grandma was fine. The doctor was wrecked! They had not thought of a name. So as I stumbled out, soaked to the skin, and joints stiff from kneeling, they agreed on 'Dr John' for a name. I think that was really his name for the first day! In due course he was embraced into his family and re-named. But God had truly done something amazing that night!

Five loaves and two fishes

Guyana has an Amazonian interior. Travelling to some interior Amerindian villages that were not served by rivers required an army lorry with church benches strapped to the back. We needed to take fresh water with us which we rationed carefully. We travelled with a chainsaw and frequently needed to use this to remove fallen trees from the jungle track that we were travelling along. In villagers like 72 miles (so called because it is 72 miles from Georgetown) we might have been 400 miles away due to the difficult terrain. The journey usually took between 8 and 10 hours.

Years earlier when we went on the rivers I became increasingly concerned with the safety of travelling as the boat we used was far from robust. So we set about raising funds in England to have a safer boat built. People were generous and we were able to commission a new boat together with a powerful new outboard motor, life jackets, and waterproof covering to give some protection from the tropical rain. It was capable of carrying eight people and their bags.

As a result we were now able to visit remote Amerindian communities such as *Yarakita, Honida, Wauna, and Kaituma.* One particular instance stands out in my mind as demonstrating the divine protection the father gives us. We had been several hours up river, again in the village of Micobi. Even in the new

Five loaves and two fishes

boat it was a five hour journey home. For one good reason after another good reason we left a little later than planned.

On the way we stopped briefly at a logging compound. Men would live there for weeks on end, deep into mosquito saturated jungle. We found many of the workers were sick with malaria. So we spent over an hour treating them all, and praying with those who wanted. When we got back on the river we had a four hour journey to get back to Bartica before nightfall. But it was 3pm, and darkness falls like a curtain at 6pm. Worse still, before Bartica there are rapids, and the experienced captains could only navigate this is good light. Passing over the rapids after nightfall was not permitted, and practically impossible. Rocks protruded in many places over a significant stretch of the river, the water racing this way and that, and sinister life waiting below the surface for any who would enter.

The journey was fine until darkness fell. At 6pm the sun's light faded and by 6.15pm it was pitch dark. We are used to city darkness, which is not really dark. But in the rural tropics it is totally black. We knew the rapids were ahead of us, and began to hear the crashing sounds coming from them. One of the team went to the front of the boat and began to worship God with her lovely voice. I prayed, fearing I had

Five loaves and two fishes

taken my team into a completely unnecessary, and probably lethal situation.

Suddenly the sky lit up with tropical lightning. For a brief moment, everything was visible. The captain saw the rapids, and his experienced eye took the boat through the known safe passage. However there were three rapids. But each time we approached them the sky would light up and the captain would see the safe passage. And so we returned safely to Bartica under the protection of God.

Once home we praised God for the experience. I was certain he wanted me to know he was not impressed with my team leading and decision-making, but that as he had more work for us all to do he had stepped in. And I was grateful.

As the years passed we travelled to the places that were most poor. Mabaruma was one such place. It was at the most westerly border of Guyana, very close to Venezuela. Travel was by sea from Georgetown, taking 24 hours, or by a small aircraft taking the pilot and 9 people over the jungle. On one occasion we went as a team of four, taking all our medicines and equipment with us.

We had a fruitful time, travelling on many unmade roads, and living in fairly basic homes. On the way

Five loaves and two fishes

back we got to the small airport early. I say airport, but it was just a sun-baked mud strip. I felt sure all would be well. But the procedures were different to all I knew. On registration with the official, who turned up about 30 minutes before the flight was due, it became clear that each passenger was to be weighed together with his or her luggage, and there was an absolute maximum for the flight. We had a fairly slim team, and about 30kg of medicines. Just then the local midwife turned up to fly back. She was big, maybe even huge. My heart sank. Shortly after, the official informed us all that we were 30kg over weight. I looked at the midwife. Then I looked at my medicines, and I knew what would happen. My medicines were left behind. I collected them two years later.

But God has a sense of humour. The seats were arranged in pairs to the left, then a single to the right in three rows. My allocated seat was against the window in the pair, and guess what - yes the midwife was next to me. I did not have sufficient space to breathe properly until the flight landed and we all disembarked!

We visited Guyana again in 2008 with another team. The journey involved a transit through Barbados before flying on to Guyana. I was coming through customs in Barbados with a large case of medicines,

Five loaves and two fishes

purchased in the UK. In those days it was hard to get quality medicines locally, so we imported them. Now we buy most of our high volume medicines in the country being visited.

I had completed a customs declaration, but knew that I was likely to be stopped and questioned. There was the possibility of having my precious cargo confiscated. Or worse. Bribes were expected. Immediately ahead of me was one of our team. She was wearing army fatigue trousers. None of us knew that these are banned for civilian use in Barbados.

We approached the customs official holding out our declarations. Hers was blank. Mine contained an extensive drug inventory. As she approached, the official became very animated, pulling her to one side and pushing her into an adjacent changing area, telling her that she must remove the fatigues and put on more suitable clothing. With no concern about me, he waived me through, intent on dealing with the trouser reprobate. And so our medicines arrived safely. The Lord of Heaven's Armies was, once again on our case.

Five loaves and two fishes

Chapter 5 - Getting serious - John

In 1998 I moved into a Divisional Medical Director role in Leeds, at the Leeds Teaching Hospitals NHS Trust - one of Europe's largest hospitals. It was a time of discovery and challenge. I had never really considered how far I wanted to pursue my UK career. But at the same time the overseas opportunities were developing. And to be honest they had my prime attention. Back at base I became responsible for over 120 fellow consultants, trying to balance their needs against the needs of the service.

Over the next 2 years I was a medical director, a consultant, a pastor, a missionary, a husband and a Dad. Now you don't need a lot of insight or wisdom to calculate that would not be sustainable for long. I was working on overload. I used to meet colleagues in the corridor and they would refer to some event which I could not recall at all. Sometimes I struggled to remember what their names were, or what had been discussed with whom. Or when. Eventually I realised that although the human brain is fairly amazing, it can't do the impossible. Certainly mine couldn't.

So in 2000 I went to see my boss, the overall Trust Medical Director. He was a great chap, unusually pastoral for a medical leader. We got on well. I told him I really could not continue to do justice to my job

Five loaves and two fishes

as Divisional Medical Director. I recall the meeting very well. He asked me what I really wanted to do. And here was one of those key moments. Time stops, the angels watch, and heaven waits.

I was actually helped as, at that moment I saw an image of a dove over his head. I know that sounds strange, but I really did. And the dove gave me a lot of courage because you don't see doves in hospital offices often. So I said I really wanted to start an overseas project within the hospital, and I could lead it. From my boss's reaction it was as if I had said something ordinary, like I wanted to go to a restaurant tonight. He just said, yes, why not? And one of the early "institutional" National Health Service hospital overseas links was born.

It was about overseas. And partnering. And training too. So we called it the "Overseas Partnering and Training Initiative". Since no-one could remember the name, it was shortened to OPTIN. All staff were invited to opt in, and many did. We formed a charity and raised funds for the cause. It connected with many.

Rosie soon became a key ally. She was a sonographer (a person skilled in carrying out ultrasound scans) but she also lectured at the University and was rather expert at both. We became friends and, as is often the

Five loaves and two fishes

case in such partnerships, we played off each others's strengths. She had already pioneered ultrasound projects in Uganda single handedly. In terms of capacity building and creating sustainable projects (buzz words in this field) she had it sorted.

Around this time I met Cy Chadwick. He had come through TV ranks, initially as an actor in the "Emmerdale" series. Following this he had established his own film production company. When we met, he wanted to create a reality series on the Leeds A&E service. It was not easy to get all my colleagues on board, but another of my fellow consultants was also keen. We were probably the most vocal, so we carried the day. Wayne is a Welsh man, used to speaking his mind, and a very expert emergency physician. So the TV series was broadcast. One of us apparently came over as Clooney, though to this day I am unsure which. The series built and the Yorkshire residents had a diet of us for a while. One of the profound benefits for me was watching Cy doing video editing. He showed me how it was done, and I watched in awe.

Of course, lives rub off against each other and OPTIN fascinated Cy. There was a new project looking hopeful in Bangladesh. Our physiotherapist friend, Phil, was working at the famous Centre for the Rehabilitation of the Paralysed (CRP), in Dhaka. I

Five loaves and two fishes

went to visit. It was soon clear that the spinal unit was the only one catering for over 100 million people. All the patients, most of whom were paralysed from the neck down, were nursed on traction for six weeks. They were turned every two hours to avoid pressure sores. To see dozens like this was a wretched sight. They were usually young men and women, with flaccid, helpless bodies and double incontinence. After the six weeks their bones would be healed, though the spinal cord damage would never heal. But they could then be strapped in chairs and start their new, massively changed, lives.

One of my friends back home, Jake Timothy, was a Neurosurgeon specialising in Spinal Surgery. I knew that he and his colleagues could operate on these poor folk, and get them mobilised in chairs within days. This meant that the physiotherapists could get their joints moving to prevent stiffness and contractures. So we started the spinal surgery project and, over time, Jake and three other spinal surgeons visited the centre. Drills and jigs, titanium plates and screws were donated. When they ran out, everything was copied and made locally. Over the space of two years all existing and new patients were operated on. Previously none were. The transformation was profound. The beds used for turning became redundant. The length of stay plummeted, and patients were even flown in from several other Asian

Five loaves and two fishes

nations for spinal surgery. We never anticipated such a massive effect.

On one visit I met a paralysed man, who was wheelchair bound. He had travelled over 6 days by bus from Nepal to be at a Spinal Injuries Conference held at CRP. When I say by bus, I don't mean a First Bus Company or a Greyhound coach. I mean a worn out, rough, black smoke-coughing machine that had been welded in so many places that there were few original bodywork parts.

The conference lasted 3 days, and then he travelled back the same way. He had little money, poor health and few comforts. But the prize of learning how a Spinal Injuries Unit runs, and taking this to Nepal, filled his mind. God spoke to me through him. The fact is we will undertake any journey if we see the benefit. Perseverance is less to do with character and more to do with vision. How we need to grasp a real vision.

Cy got wind of the project at CRP and proposed another series called "Flying Doctor". So I went with Cy and Kevin, his sound engineer. At CRP we captured the story on film. The people of Yorkshire were subjected to 5 minutes every tea-time of the flying doctor. In fact it was an amazing testimony to God's grace. The dove I had seen must have been real.

Five loaves and two fishes

In 2002 Rosie wanted me to go to Uganda with her to see the Ultrasound project she had started in Kamuli. In hindsight, we did not plan this carefully, we just went. I now see a lot of people doing that. Its not a great plan, and it is much better to be clear and strategic in the mission objective. But there we were in Kamuli Hospital, one of the 50 or so NGO (non governmental organisation) hospitals in Uganda. The work at Kamuli Hospital was run by a team of Catholic nuns. I recall an experience there that chilled and changed me. It had been over 10 years since I had carried out any serious surgery. One day a young man, a teacher in his early 20's, was brought in. He was vomiting blood, almost certainly from a bleeding duodenal ulcer. The procedure for blood transfusion was to test the patient's group, then buy blood for $10 a pint from locals who would be HIV tested first. I ran around buying blood from the locals. I knew I should operate on him but I had lost my confidence. The hours passed, and before sunset, so did he. The loss of a vital teacher was bad enough, but for it to have been avoidable was crushing. It was another learning moment. I resolved that never again would I let this happen.

The ultrasound machine was in regular use by a couple of people Rosie had trained. It was great to see, but we decided we needed to spread the effect.

Five loaves and two fishes

We went east to the Government hospital in the town of Mbale where they had shown some interest. What we saw there horrified us - young patients neglected and surgeons busy in private practice. So we left and went north to the old leprosy hospital at Kumi. We subsequently built a fruitful tele-medicine project there. The government hospitals had a different code to the non-governmental organisations, most of which are Christian. We learned this first-hand. We also learned to plan visits carefully, not just because they are expensive in terms of time, energy and money but also because of the missed opportunities resulting from not doing so.

During 2002 a tragedy struck. A small team from Leeds arrived in Uganda and were being collected from the airport. Somehow the minibus was involved in a collision. The driver and the hospital's only surgeon were killed. The visiting sonographer was left on the roadside, bleeding and seriously injured. People often wonder why we are cautious about casual medical tourism. The fact is that it is dangerous. The roads pose the biggest risk to health and welfare. We have now seen too many such tragedies. Visitors need to know this, and be prepared. Or maybe stay at home and offer prayer and funds.

That year I had the privilege of meeting Lord Swinfen, who had put personal funds into a trust to facilitate

Five loaves and two fishes

telemedicine projects. He had helped fund the Kumi link, and he invited me to have tea with him in the House of Lords. Sitting there I smiled when I thought how God works. And I thought about the dove.

I also met Eldryd Parry who had founded the Tropical Health and Education Trust (THET). I made an appointment and met this wonderful godly man. He had spent his life in Africa as a Professor of Medicine, using his life and skills to bless the people. His organisation is now a major governmental conduit for overseas medical aid, but then it was fairly rudimentary. He has since been knighted, has an OBE, and has a lifetime of academic African experience to reflect upon. But he has been an inspiration to many, me included.

Later that year an interesting event occurred. My good friend Wayne, the Welsh doctor, became aware that his mum was suffering from lung cancer. She was a good chapel-attending woman, and, much to his embarrassment, she asked if Myra and I would pray for her. The day Wayne called was not a good one. Myra and I argue every eclipse of the sun, which is approximately every 20 years. But we had argued that day. Then we received the telephone call from Wayne asking us to pray with his Mum.

Five loaves and two fishes

We would have been willing to pray for sinusitis. Or a common cold. Or maybe backache. Category B stuff was fine. But Wayne's Mum had lung cancer. And to the informed, it was a pleomorphic, anaplastic type. That is among the worst. In the words of the late AA Gill, "the full english breakfast". A healing definitely would be category A.

Now why would God embarrass us like that? The convergence of a row and the need for a category A healing had the effect that we felt totally inadequate. But it also had the effect that we had absolutely no confidence in any ability within ourselves. But we duly went to the house and took Sheila into the dining room. There were just the three of us. And we laid hands on her, anointed her with oil, and prayed.

Now, the reality of the kingdom (and I am too old to deal with make-believe) is often not a lot happens when we do this. However, from time to time, amazing things _do_ happen. Otherwise we would all stop praying for healing. And that day, an amazing thing happened. Sheila told us she felt heat in her left chest and left arm. The cancer was in the left chest. She was not tutored to say this. She had definitely not been to New Wine, Soul Survivor, or attended a John Wimber conference. God was obviously at work. We finished praying, our row far in the distance, and we realised God was in this. Sure enough, as the weeks

Five loaves and two fishes

passed, the chest x-rays showed the mass getting smaller. It had been the size of an orange, and it shrank to the size of an almond. The specialist cancer doctors could not account for her improvement.

The problem was that Sheila could not relax into Father's plan. She remained so anxious, and even as the cancer shrunk, she faded emotionally and in her spirit. And one night, she slept and did not wake up. Even today, many years later, I can't work it out. All I can do is report the facts as I saw them. And as a doctor, I have to report that in almost 40 years I have not heard of such a cancer shrinking.

Following God is full of mystery. I suppose it is meant to be like that, otherwise we would have him in a box. And the 'Lord of heaven's armies' can't fit in a box.

Five loaves and two fishes

Chapter 6 - Taking bigger risks - Myra

My first trip to the island of Mindanao, the most southerly of the Philippines archipelago, was as formative as our first medical mission to Guyana. I had been planning a third mission to Guyana when God redirected me in a way I don't often experience. We were at the national conference of Connections UK, which linked so many little rural churches across the globe, when I found myself chatting to another GP over coffee. He was telling me no medical doctor had been to a certain area in Mindanao for years and the leader of the churches there was desperate for someone to go. My heart began pounding and I felt like a heavenly lottery hand was pointing a large finger directly over my head. I'm not someone who is often so absolutely sure of myself but I knew before the end of the day I would be going to the Philippines the same autumn.

I spoke with a salty dog of many missions to the Philippines called Allan Cameron. He has now gone to be with his precious Jesus but his big heart and love for the Philippino people was infectious. He put me in touch with a lady from Birmingham who had been once before and felt burdened to return. She recruited her good friend, Mary to come. Meanwhile I co-opted Becci, now 18 years old, who was on a gap year and bursting to come with me.

Five loaves and two fishes

Audrey's heart was to do a women's conference and we planned to minister for 3 days to all the pastors' wives and associates before starting 10 days of medical outreach. We were a motley crew with little preaching experience but we were all willing and prepared to make mistakes, which is all the Master requires.

The pastor we would work with was Bonifacio Sembran who became a dear and precious friend, with whom we shared many adventures. He had started life as an angry young man who got himself into many scrapes as a result of his temper. The life-changing event for him was his involvement in a fight where he almost killed a man and went on the run from the police. When he was caught and brought to trial, Boni's father pleaded with the judge to give him a chance, and present to Boni a choice between bible school and prison. No doubt Boni was aware of the notoriously awful conditions in Mindanao's jails and not surprisingly he chose the former. Within a few months Jesus had captured his heart and transformed his life. He met the lovely Odette who became not only his wife but his best friend and partner in mission for the next four decades. Together they founded a bible school and planted over 160 churches installing their new graduates as pastors each time a new church was formed.

Five loaves and two fishes

Boni was an incredible visionary in practical as well as spiritual realms. He took on managing land parcels the government was leasing out and planted trees which are now supplying wood for the churches being constructed around the area. He grew food to feed his family and the bible students. He farmed pigs so each new pastor could have a piglet to breed from. He took his place in the local community and became a trusted friend of governors and army generals but he also made enemies among the Muslim rebels as a result of his gospel activity. This earned him a place as number two on their death list. In his time at Ipil he had a permanent army guard stationed at his home 24/7.

The town of Ipil is on the edge of Muslim held rebel territory and was subject to a terrible massacre in 1997. The rebels entered the town on a busy market day and opened fire indiscriminately in the market place. One hundred and sixty people died that day.

We were aware of all the facts prior to our mission and were told we would have an armed guard. Allan was reassuring. While many people had stopped going he had continued to visit giving support and encouragement to the bible students and the work of outreach. He was affectionately known as Lolo (grandad) Allan, or the apostle to the Philippines.

There was a UK conference just prior to our visit with amazing speakers from all over the world. As I considered what we were about to embark on I felt

Five loaves and two fishes

very inadequate. I can remember crying in the ladies toilet and wondering what on earth I was getting into, feeling completely out of my depth. It was not helped by the fact we were only about 4 weeks after the tragedies of 9/11 and the foreign office was warning against any travel to the Philippines, especially Mindanao. My parents were horrified I still planned to go and take our beautiful young daughter with me but I KNEW God had called me and there was no going back.

We assembled at Audrey's house on the afternoon of the flight waiting for Mary to arrive but instead there came a phone call to say her unbelieving husband didn't want her to go and she had unpacked her case. He had berated her with his worries and she felt unable to go against his wishes despite the fact she often had to worry about him on recreational sailing trips around the world. We three were devastated we had lost a precious team member but prayed and committed our trip into Father's hands. Ten minutes before we left for the airport Mary rang back to say Alan had relented, her bag was re packed and she was on her way!

The flight to Paris was delayed and we arrived with very little time to make our connection. We were told we could get across the airport if we hurried but our bags would not make it! This was a disaster because all the medicines were in our cases and we could not

Five loaves and two fishes

wait in Manila for them to arrive 2 days later on the next Air France flight. We thought quickly and asked if there was another flight route which would allow us to wait for the bags and have them with us in Manila. The lady on the transfer desk was incredibly sweet and helpful. She re routed us via Japan and gave us a few hours in a nearby hotel while we waited. We had a chance encounter in the hotel lobby with a lady burdened with guilt. As we shared the love of Jesus she met our precious Saviour and left with my pocket New Testament in her hands! Maybe our delay had been just for her!

We were beyond tired after our roundabout flight followed directly by the internal flight down to Mindanao. The weight of our bags was more than double our allowance but I naively produced a letter from the Governor of Zamboango province, Mindanao which Boni had supplied beforehand, complete with red wax seal. We were waved through without charge. We were trying to cling to our suitcases at Dipolog airport despite the attempts of many baggage handlers to wrest them from our grasp when Boni's son and driver arrived to whisk us away for the 3 hour drive south to Ipil. We arrived late at night to a welcome fit for royalty and garlands of flowers were wrapped around each of our necks.

The Sembran household and extended families, ministries and spheres of influence were all run with

Five loaves and two fishes

great precision by the teamwork of Boni and Odette. It was soon clear people were arriving for a well planned conference. Not a "ladies" conference as we had envisaged but a full blown annual gathering for about 100 pastors in the locality and far flung places of the island with us as the main speakers! Yes, the only "ladies" bit about the conference was the four of us!

We sang, Becci danced, we told stories and "preached". Miraculously these godly, experienced men and women were blessed and encouraged by our five loaves and two fishes. Amazingly they asked us to come back the following year!

The days were busy doing medical outreach because we had to travel up to two hours each way at times and Boni did not like us to be out after dark for security reasons. We usually had three young soldiers with us and the day we did a clinic for the army camp, they fetched us in one of their armoured vehicles. It was like an oven on wheels and we begged to do the return journey in a jeep with Boni riding shotgun!

As the only medic I was seeing over 100 people each day but the rest of the team worked really hard with crowd control and pharmacy so somehow we managed to see all who came for help. Those beyond the scope of my bag of medicines went to the prayer team. We saw miracles. A deaf man started hearing again, a breast lump shrank and a young man with polio brought on a buffalo cart got up and walked. We

Five loaves and two fishes

somehow found time in each day to speak about the love of Jesus as well as demonstrate it and Boni confirmed in the months following all of his churches had grown. This resonated with the verses given by a friend the day before we left, "Wherever you place your feet I will give you the ground". The whole time we were there I felt as if I was on a tandem bike with Jesus and he was doing all the peddling. It was such an exhilarating ride.

We were so sad at the end to leave our new friends. I exacted from Boni the promise we would leave for the flight in English not Philippino time and we set off early for the flight at 1300 hours. Arriving at Dipolog in good time we meandered into town for some food. There is not much at Dipolog airport except a one room waiting area.

It was strangely quiet as we pulled up to the terminal and the officials looked at us with some puzzlement. "Today's flight has already gone" they said. "It's the first day of the change to winter scheduling". Our hearts sank as we realised our plane had been taxiing down the runway as we sat in ignorance eating an early lunch. There would be no more flights for 24 hours and the Air France flights from Manila did not fly every day so it would be a three day delay in getting home. We asked all sorts of questions about getting to another airport by road or sea but it was all too late except.... I found the words leaving my mouth before I

Five loaves and two fishes

had time to think... "can we charter a plane?" The answer was "yes" and initially we miscalculated the cost with the exchange rate. When we realised the true cost of £600 our hearts were too far down the road of wanting to get home and we rationalised £150 for a pleasure flight in a small plane would have to do as our Christmas present for the year! The problem was we had no money and none of our credit cards worked at the banks. Boni's resourceful son, Joshua, had now entered into the adventure and we set off to find a Pastor friend of his father's who also ran a business. Though he had never laid eyes on us before, he lent us the money there and then!

We dashed back to the airport and ordered the plane to take us to the airport on the next island where we could pick up a connecting flight to Manila. The wait was interminable and time seemed to be running late as the light started to fade and a dot appeared on the horizon. The dot grew as it came in to land but it really was a small plane. The pilot looked suspiciously at our luggage as we all climbed aboard over the wing of the 5 seater. I was dubious when Becci sat next to the pilot and he handed her the map. She was magnificent at many things, but map reading was not among them. I decided at this point if my life ended I was actually ready for heaven.

The flight was really spectacular as we flew low over thousands of tiny islands with fishing nets, like spiders

Five loaves and two fishes

webs, visible in the sea. As the sun was setting we reached the island of Cebu, an electric storm raging around us. We landed safely and taxied to the light aircraft hangar. The reality suddenly dawned on all of us the commercial airport was on the other side of an extensive runway. It seemed we were so near but so far and the clock was ticking on the flight to Manila. Our Heavenly Father stepped in again and prompted the kindly Japanese pilot to lend us both his car and his own driver to take us by road to the terminal building. I never cease to be amazed by the generosity of complete strangers and hope I will always be ready to be the answer to someone else's prayer in time of need. The journey seemed endless as we had to circumnavigate the periphery of the whole airport and I did wonder at one point if we were being kidnapped and driven to a meet a horrible fate. The driver was, however, faithful and deposited us at the door refusing all payment for his trouble. Our flight was being called as we ran through the airport and finally sank into our seats on board the flight to Manila.

Looking back now I realise the trip was one of the most exciting times of my life in which I was so fully thrown on God and out of my depth I could only let go and be carried where the water took me.

On my second visit to Mindanao in 2002, Tim, now in medical school, accompanied me, together with another GP. The mission to a remote mountain village

Five loaves and two fishes

was considered dangerous by the army chief so instead of the usual 3 guards, a lorry with 12 soldiers conveyed the team. In his words "it is easier to protect you than to rescue you".

After 2 hours of travelling on muddy roads we arrived and set up consultations under the trees. Tim brought his first patient to his mother for advice. She had a hideous foul smelling mushroom-like tumour on the back of her head which had been growing for months. She looked downcast and dejected. She had travelled miles to the nearest hospital and been told it would cost £1,000 for its removal. This was a king's ransom for her.

Dr Gordon, the other GP, and Myra consulted and felt something had to be done for the poor lady. So a trestle table in the shade of the trees became an operating theatre but also a theatre where the white people provided a scene of entertainment for all the watching bible students, children, villagers and soldiers. After some pain relieving tablets and an injection of local anaesthetic she looked at us with hopeless blackness in her eyes and willingly lay face down on the table.

With a small sterile dressing pack and a few instruments we struggled to remove the offending lesion and control the bleeding. A headband of crepe bandage stemmed the oozing but it was no sooner applied than a tropical rainstorm began and we all had

Five loaves and two fishes

to run for shelter in the church. I looked at our patient and saw a new look of hope in her eyes as if Jesus had met her spirit while she submitted herself to the white strangers, as she lay on the wooden table.

We had an impromptu worship service which lifted us all into the spirit and was one of those glimpses "beyond the veil" to what worship in heaven might be like. I observed Carol during our time of worship, partly because she had lost a good deal of blood and I was worried she might faint! She appeared to be truly at peace and set free.

A year or so later I was back in Mindanao with John and at the usual Pastor's Conference, where the white people were expected to do all the preaching. Carol's pastor came to tell us of the great transformation in her life. "She is one of my best church members and as a result of her healing my church has doubled in size". We were astounded. What he also told us was she had been so desperate and so depressed by her physical condition, she had been planning to take her own life that very week. We stood in awe of God's grace and mercy.

In 2010 we were again doing a medical mission with a different team. I was unaware we were near Carol's home village but news had reached her so she had taken a motorbike taxi down the mountain to come to the clinic. I was overwhelmed by the joy of seeing her again and hardly recognised her. She was confident

Five loaves and two fishes

and composed with a sense of God's spirit radiating from her life. She had outlived both her pastor and his wife and was taking a major role in the leadership of the church.

When we are obedient to His leading we are unable to foresee the outcomes He sees, but what a joy to be part of His plan for someone's life. We had given our loaves and fishes and seen an amazing multiplication unfold.

Five loaves and two fishes

Chapter 7 – More of the Philippines - Myra

On the 2005 trip to the Philippines we were able to go together accompanied by Audrey who had been with me in 2001. Since the previous trips Pastor Boni had relocated to the port of Dipolog as the army no longer felt able to give him adequate security in Ipil where the rebel situation had deteriorated. We undertook the usual daily medical missions and saw many people giving their hearts to Jesus as various members of the team shared the gospel of love.

As with every mission the sickest patients always appear at the end of the clinic or at some other time after it finishes. And so it was on this mission, one Sunday morning we looked across at the end of the service to see a girl approaching with an enormous swelling of her thyroid. We could readily see the classic signs of gross over activity in the gland. She was in a very advanced phase with severe heart failure. This 21 year old girl was going to die within weeks. For the price of a daily cup of coffee we were able to give her a supply of tablets to calm her thyroid and heart rate. She had previously been on treatment but when her father died she had no longer been able to afford the tablets. We gave funds to the pastor for the monitoring of her condition.

A year later when we returned she was a different girl. Not only was she physically changed, but her whole

Five loaves and two fishes

outlook and demeanour were transformed. She greeted us with a big smile and told us how her life was back on track. We discovered that she had been so desperate, that like the lady with the scalp growth, she had been planning her suicide. Now she was reading her bible and following her Jesus. She had sold a chicken to pay for the two hour bus journey to meet us.

In 2006 our faithful mission partner, Deloris, was able to join us again, and we also took an intrepid spinster in her mid 70's who really felt God had called her to go. She was not a well lady and within a year had gone home to be with her Saviour. As a Sunday school teacher over at least 6 decades she was a great hit with all the children.

Our flight was from Manchester to Manila via Amsterdam. We then would have the onward flight to the southern Philippine city of Dipolog. At Amsterdam we had a short transit time and when we reached the gate we found that the flight was overbooked. To our horror we were told we would not be on it. We pleaded with the air hostess as the internal flights in the Philippines were infrequent and we would have lost several days of mission if forced to fly the next day. She asked us to take a seat and we went away to pray. Other passengers were going through to the plane and we continued to wait for some 20 minutes,

Five loaves and two fishes

praying with fervour. Then just as most people were on board the hostess came to us and with a smile and wink she led us onto the plane. Once again our Father was in control!

On our arrival in Dipolog we were desperate to see Amette, pastor Boni's daughter in law. There had been many phone calls and emails between us regarding a huge swelling in the bone on her left thigh that had caused a fracture. It sounded very serious and it was most likely that she had an aggressive cancer of the femur. This was also the opinion of the local specialists. The family had taken her to the nearest major hospital on the next island where she was booked for a hind quarter amputation. This is unimaginably worse than an amputation of the leg because it is done at the level of the hip. We were heartbroken as we thought of the effect on the life of this young mother of four.

We entered the room to find her lying on the bed with a large metal frame on her leg. There had been no amputation! She proceeded to tell us the story. As they had journeyed by boat to Cebu Island her four year old son became increasingly distressed and unable to face the prospect of his mother losing her leg. He then laid his hands on the swollen thigh and prayed aloud with great fervour that she would be healed. Amette was sure she then saw a cross in the

Five loaves and two fishes

sky. She did not know what was going to happen, but she experienced great peace from that time on. They reached the hospital and she was booked for the operation at 8am the next morning. The morning of her surgery the head surgeon overslept and was caught up in terrible traffic. This meant he didn't feel able to fit in what would have been a four hour operation and instead he opted to do biopsies of the affected area to assess the exact nature of the tumour.

To everyone's amazement the small procedure revealed a large collection of pus in the bone but no sign of cancer. The surgeon's late arrival had saved her leg! It took many months of treatment and wearing of the brace before the infection was cleared and her bone finally healed. Within 2 years, however, she was back dancing on the stage and leading the church in worship.

As I already said the sickest patients appear at all times of day and night. So it was one breakfast time that a mother brought a three year old boy who had injured his eye with a bamboo stick. It had pierced his eyeball one week earlier. The situation caused our hearts to sink because his eye had become infected and visibly filled with pus. The worst part of this situation is that the infection can track through the optic nerve and cause blindness in the other eye as well.

Five loaves and two fishes

We felt entirely helpless and a conversation with our son Tim (who has expertise in infections, training as a microbiology specialist) confirmed our worst fears for this child. We gave some antibiotic eye ointment which was the equivalent of a sticking plaster on a gaping wound and then we laid hands on him and prayed.

Can you imagine our consternation the next day when the child was in church running around happily? When we examined him he was seeing perfectly with both eyes. Our father had healed him in a most amazing way. We have never heard of such a recovery, and the books would say it is impossible.

It had always been our pattern in the Philippines to arrive in a village with the team of bible students and say a few words before starting clinic. Sometimes we would preach and the students would lead worship or other times we would break for lunch and have singing and preaching before continuing to treat the sick. We often used childrens' songs with actions as these were always a good way of involving the villagers. Filipinos are warm, fun loving people who enjoy participating. On this mission in 2006 we began to use "Our God is a great big God" written by our friend Nigel Hemming. It was an instant success with the locals and several "encores" were always required! More surprisingly it seems that hearts were opened

Five loaves and two fishes

dramatically by this simple song and in every village where we used the song we saw dozens of people coming forward to accept Jesus into their lives.

Pastor Boni's son Joshua and his wife Amette live in Gatas approximately an hour from Dipolog. They met and married very young. I first got to know them in 2001. At the age of 20 they had 2 small children and were looking after 16 orphans in a few mud huts each with a roof of banana leaves which all leaked whenever it rained. Despite the poor conditions the children were happy and knew they were loved. They woke every morning at 5am to do their share of household jobs such as cleaning up and fetching water. Then they had a time of worship and prayer before breakfast and school. Some of them had one living parent but if a man loses his wife he can't care for children and work. There were two little girls whose mother had died and their father worked in the local market for a pittance. They had been living on water for several weeks. When Joshua and Amette brought them to Gatas she overheard them say to one another "Look, now we can eat!"

The following year with generous gifts from the UK, work on a new orphanage building began so that within a couple of years the children had proper rooms and beds as well as toilet and washing facilities. Many of these children have a real and living faith

Five loaves and two fishes

which would be a challenge to those of us brought up in much more comfortable situations. In later years some of those who had grown up in Gatas went on to attend Pastor Boni's bible school and become pastors in his network of churches.

It was during one of our mission days in the Gatas orphanage that we met a lady with a severely infected foot. Like many of the poor Filipinos she walked barefoot and had trodden on a piece of sharp bamboo. An infection developed which festered. She experienced increasing pain, then a large collection of pus formed. The infection had escalated until the entire foot was desperately swollen, red and hot. She was on the brink of getting widespread sepsis which is universally fatal without treatment.

John had been using ketamine regularly in our overseas missions as it's a quick acting and safe anaesthetic. She was well anaesthetised as John made a big hole in her foot to adequately drain all the pus and stop it reforming. One of the problems with ketamine in adults is the confusion it causes as patients wake. This lady had a very florid reaction as the ketamine was wearing off. She was convinced that John was a white devil and screamed loudly about this for several minutes! The next day her opinion was different and she thought he was an angel who had

Five loaves and two fishes

saved her life. She became a faithful member of Joshua and Amette's new church.

Not all our encounters with sick people had happy endings. At the same clinic as the lady with the infected foot, we saw a 11 year old girl in heart failure brought by her grandmother. She had suffered an episode of rheumatic fever following a throat infection some weeks previously. Had we seen her at the time a few doses of penicillin would have saved her heart and her life. Sadly she was in extremis and fighting for her breath. We had to explain the awful prognosis to her and grandma. They accepted the reality without any tears or drama. They left quietly after prayer, with a supply of medication to bring some relief of her symptoms. We heard that she died 3 weeks later.

The decade we had spent working with Pastor Boni had been a joy and an inspiration. He was a larger than life character with a big heart for God and a great love for people. His desire to see others find the Jesus he knew and loved was the driving passion of his life. His incredible far-sightedness and vision had enabled him to start with one church but go on to plant many more and start a bible school. In this way he trained pastors for the 160 churches he would plant in his lifetime.

Five loaves and two fishes

When he developed liver cancer in 2011 we spent hours on the phone trying to advise the family and speaking with the doctors in Cebu. The tumours were inoperable and probably due to hepatitis B, contracted decades earlier, and so prevalent in the Philippines. He returned to Mindanao to be cared for by his family. His daughter, Joyce, a qualified nurse, looked after him until the end. He fought bravely and gave a powerful testimony to his hope in eternity only weeks before he died in October 2011. We were so sad not to have seen him to say goodbye and did not get to Dipolog until a month after he died. It was humbling to be woken on the morning of November 1st (all souls day) to lead the prayers with the bible students and his family. As we gathered at his grave the words of Hebrews 12 came to mind. ...

> *Therefore since we are surrounded by so great a cloud of witnesses, we must get rid of every weight and the sin that clings so closely, and run with endurance the race set out for us, keeping our eyes fixed on Jesus, the pioneer and perfecto of our faith. For the joy set out before him he endured the cross, despising the shame, and has taken his seat at the right hand of the throne of God.*

As we remembered a man who had lived well in the service of others we prayed that we would have the courage to follow his example as he now is part of that

Five loaves and two fishes

"great cloud of witnesses" watching from heaven and cheering us on in our feeble efforts.

We returned to Mindanao the following spring to continue our support of Boni's grieving family. Audrey, from Birmingham, joined us again and brought great comfort to Boni's widow Odete with many hugs and times of prayer. We encouraged all the family to allow the flow of tears they had been stoically holding back.

Boni's oldest son, Joshua, who had always appeared so quiet and reserved was stepping into the very large boots of his father. He seemed to have the respect and support of the network of pastors many of whom were decades older than him. Odette was doing her best to lead the church at Dipolog in the in the midst of her profound grief. She had Boni had been so close since the time they fell in love at bible school. They had been utterly devoted to each other and their common purpose in the kingdom. They had been parents to so many young bible students who had grown up under their discipleship which was characterised by great love and tough discipline.

Joshua had inherited his father's passion for expanding God's work especially amongst the poorest and most needy. The network of churches extended not only to the immediate area but to some places two hundred

Five loaves and two fishes

miles away. He and Amete began travelling hundreds of miles to support and encourage existing churches as well as seeking to plant new ones. Despite advice to avoid pregnancy after her leg problems Amete conceived and gave birth to a beautiful little girl who is much loved by the four older brothers. They often travel with one or all of the children in tow. The boys had frequently been involved in our medical teams and helped count tablets or take blood pressures!

Joshua expressed a desire to visit a mountain village close to the areas where the muslim rebels were operating. The local mayor was due to go with an army escort and we were offered a lift in their convoy. It seems no white people had been to this village and Joshua wanted to hold a medical clinic with a view to church planting. The rains had been very heavy and the mud was nearly a foot deep on some of the tracks up to the village. The lorry was 6x6 not 4x4 but even so we had to get out several times to reduce the weight. We finally reached the village of Guibo late in the morning and were greeted with a fantastic lunch laid on for the team. The lady mayor had gained much credibility with the locals for her hard work and integrity during her short time in office. She was keen to visit the next village 5 miles further and promised to return in the lorry at 4pm for the return journey.

Five loaves and two fishes

We embarked on a medical clinic and saw dozens of patients. We finished and packed up ready for the pick up at 4pm but the lorry didn't appear and we heard that the mayor and her team were stuck due to the next stretch of road becoming impassable. We waited until 5pm at which stage Joshua was anxious to get back down before dark especially as we had commitments the following day. So he hired several motorbike taxis and we set off with three people per bike and all our equipment. Unfortunately the rain got heavier and after more than an hour even penetrated even the plastic rain capes and bin bags we were wearing. The roads were worse than they had been in the morning and several times we had to get off and walk through thick mud. By the time we reached the river ford we had crossed by raft that morning we were soaked to our underwear. What Joshua had not anticipated was that the river had risen over 12 feet and was in full flood. The family who managed the raft ferry informed us that it was far too dangerous to attempt the crossing and we would need to wait until morning.

We sat on the veranda of their small shop shivering from the cold as night descended. We were about to know one of the most humbling experiences of our lives. The poor family who owned the house first brought us hot drinks and then dry clothes. An hour or so later we were blessed with a delicious hot meal and

Five loaves and two fishes

finally as the night drew on they brought us into their home and gave us their "beds" for the night. The beds were raised wooden platforms with no mattresses and we didn't sleep very much but we were so grateful to be warm and dry. The family all slept together on the floor of their living room.

The following morning we were given breakfast and we were able to bless them with an impromptu medical clinic. We gave them what little money we had as thanks for their hospitality but they were not looking for money and it was an amazing lesson in the hospitality of poverty. The waters had subsided and we were able to take the raft across, ready to continue our journey back to Dipolog.

The following week we drove several hours with an overnight stop to reach a place called Iligan which had suffered a terrible tragedy three months before with huge loss of life. The village sprawled along the border of the river and the banks of the river were linked by a concrete bridge supported on several pillars. The rains had been heavy just before the disaster so the river had been in full flood. Illegal logging was widespread in the mountainous areas upstream and water dislodged hundreds of these huge felled trees which were washed downstream. When the logs reached the bridge they became jammed effectively forming a dam behind which water built up until the pressure was so

Five loaves and two fishes

great that in the middle of the night the bridge gave way. The tumbling waters were filled with logs acting like missiles, destroying all the homes in their path. Hundreds of people were killed and bodies were washed far out to sea. Thousands were made homeless. Our charity had sent money at the time for rice and medicines. The desperate need at this time was for re-housing.

We had learned before leaving the UK that a sheet of plywood costs around £4 and on our last Sunday morning at church I was able to ask that people forgo one coffee and give the money to help rebuild a home. I left at the end of the service with several hundred pounds. So in Iligan we translated the money into sheets of plywood from a local store and set off to meet a local pastor who was trying to help those affected.

As we arrived at the church a lorry was just unloading some wood. These were the upright posts for building houses. They were overjoyed to hear that plywood was on its way to make the walls. We felt so privileged to be the answer to their prayers!

After returning from our road trip to Iligan we had a few days before the flight home and one of our day missions took us to a poor fishing village not far from Dipolog. The men were all out in the boats looking

Five loaves and two fishes

for a good catch. We parked near the beach and squeezed between several wooden shacks to wend our way to the pastor's house which was smaller than my living room and crammed with people. The children were ragged and painfully thin but their little faces shone with big smiles and laughing eyes. Those eyes were even bigger when John went off to the local bakery and returned with a huge tray of cup cakes!

It was difficult to organise a clinic in such cramped conditions but somehow we managed to see all those who were sick and check all the children and then have a worship service in this tiny place. We are humbled by people like the lady pastor of that church, working under such difficult circumstances, but caring unstintingly for her little flock.

Five loaves and two fishes

Chapter 8 - Africa! - John

I had first visited Uganda with Rosie back in 2002, and in Kamuli when I watched the young teacher fade away, I had determined that I must resurrect and use all my surgical skills. Particularly when there is no surgeon present. So I made contact with a few people and was introduced to John Craven, a retired general surgeon from York. He suggested we go out to Uganda together and operate for a couple of weeks.

And so we did. In late 2004 we flew to Uganda, and then travelled 7-8 hours north on terrible roads to the northern town of Gulu. At that time, this area was terrorised by the "Lord's Resistance Army" (LRA), led by Joseph Kony.

Kony, a member of the Acholi tribe, is the leader of the Lord's Resistance Army (LRA). He has assumed a mystical role. Since the 1990s he has kidnapped over 60,000 children, forcing the boys to become soldiers and the girls to become sex slaves. Kony initially said he fought against government oppression, but the LRA then turned against it's own supporters to "purify" the Acholi people and turn Uganda into a new kingdom based on the Ten Commandments and local Acholi traditions. He proclaimed himself the spokesperson of God at the same time being a spirit medium. He claimed to be visited by a host of spirits, including a

Five loaves and two fishes

Chinese phantom. The group is a mixture of mysticism, Acholi nationalism, and twisted biblical fundamentalism. Over two million people have been internally displaced by his indescribable activities. We saw thousands in abject poverty, living in "temporary" camps, some of which had been established over 5 years earlier.

As if this scourge was not enough, in October 2000, an outbreak of an unusual febrile illness was reported to the Ministry of Health (MoH) in Kampala by the superintendent of St. Mary's Hospital in Lacor, Gulu. It was the first outbreak of the haemorrhagic fever disease we now know as Ebola. Ebola virus infection was found not only in patients, but in some health workers at St. Mary's Hospital. Uganda rapidly learned about the epidemiology, clinical case management, and clinical treatment of Ebola. The overall death rate was over 75%, and treatment was simply supportive.

By January 2001, over 400 patients admitted to Gulu Hospital, had Ebola. The majority died. Sadly 14 of 22 health-care workers in Gulu were infected after establishing the isolation wards and most of them died. The last fatality was the godly medical superintendent who had first reported the outbreak and helped pioneer its control. He had helped the nurses to restrain a confused patient, probably becoming

Five loaves and two fishes

infected in the process. All 14 are buried at St Mary's Hospital, a testimony to the ultimate sacrifice of laying down one's life.

The chaplain at the hospital was called Elio. We have never met a chaplain like him before or since. Prior to becoming a priest he had trained as an engineer. So at St Mary's Hospital he undertook all the engineering projects. One was particularly impressive. Water is a precious commodity in most of Africa, so Elio had set up a filtration system which took all the sewerage, and progressively purified it until it was drinking water. Of course we wished we had not been told!

The LRA were active in all the villages near the hospital, and their child kidnapping tended to occur at night. As a result many families would come into the hospital compound at sunset. It was walled and gated, and offered a great deal more protection than the villages did. Children would lie on the concrete walkways, doing homework, then sleep on a single blanket. The numbers rapidly increased, and as many as 3,000 would flock into the hospital at 5pm. At the height of the troubles there were over 10,000 sleeping in tents set up in the hospital grounds. The LRA also kidnapped adults.

On one occasion, before the wall was built, they abducted several male nurses from the hospital. The

Five loaves and two fishes

hospital valued its nurses and Elio was not willing to see them abandoned to an unknown fate. He was a heavy-set man, strong from all the work he did. He left the hospital and found one of the rebel leaders. Then he made a deal. He wanted to fight the rebel leader with bare fists. If Elio lost, he would become their captive. If Elio won, the nurses would be handed back. Many onlookers were there, and the fight began. The rebel leader soon discovered his mistake. With little difficulty Elio won and the nurses were returned! It was Liberation Theology in practice!

Shortly before we arrived the LRA went into a village and abducted 40 women and children to carry supplies to their camp. They then massacred them all in cold blood. They were settling a score over the fact that ex rebels had returned to the village and been forgiven. Elio heard about it within minutes of the atrocity, and he drove to the village in his open truck. The dead were women, children and babies. They had simply been cut down with machetes. Elio took photographs of the grim scene for evidence and I have never seen such horror. Somehow there were a few still hanging onto life. Despite the rebels being nearby, with no thought of risk to himself, he used his truck to bring the living to the hospital for surgery.

In Kampala we met a pastor and his wife called Emmanuel and Florence Sunday, part of Philip

Five loaves and two fishes

Mohabir's apostolic network. We began to talk to them about the medical outreach we did in Guyana and the Philippines. They were keen to do the same in Uganda, and we shared this vision with Michael, one of the doctors working in Gulu. Our plans took shape when we returned to the UK. About nine months later we were visiting Kenya, actually taking a safari holiday to celebrate Myra's birthday. So we paid for Emmanuel, Florence and Michael to travel east to cross the border, and Myra and I journeyed west to the Kenyan town of Eldoret, where we treated our friends to a meal and a night in a hotel.

We wanted more regular outreach than simply when we were there. At the hotel we agreed the way forward. Michael would be the 'man on the ground' and form a team of local doctors and nurses. They would buy medicines locally, and visit Pastor Emmanuel's network of poor rural churches - he oversees nearly 30 - one by one. As they were all in remote village settings it was ideal. To bless Michael we agreed that we would raise funds to allow him to undertake his 3 year specialist training as a paediatrician. And so it was.

Clinics started in 2005, repeated every month, with hundreds being treated. We were so pleased that New Hope was able to function without us. The preaching of the gospel that followed each clinic ensured that

Five loaves and two fishes

many came to Christ. As before, we saw again that people who are cared for, whose needs are met, are then responsive to the gospel. Michael was so faithful and he drew in Aisha, a trained clinical support worker (half doctor, half nurse) and Frank (a junior surgeon). Frank subsequently married Lydia, a nurse. Aisha, Frank and Lydia became good friends and worked with us regularly, continuing to this day.

I recall visiting a very remote Ugandan village in 2007. Our clinics had been running for over a year, but we had not been to this place. I fact no white person had ever been to this village. We summoned patients by a village man beating a drum, and the first patient was the local witch doctor! He humbly accepted that our medicine was preferable to his, breaking the hold of decades over the villagers. Infections are hard to treat with witch doctor potions! Witch doctors are still very prevalent in Uganda, and they carry out terribly damaging 'treatments' such as pulling out healthy teeth in children, making cuts in the chests of babies, and worse.

One day a man arrived on a bicycle. He could hardly pedal as he had a horribly infected foot. It appeared that he had sustained a wooden splinter in his foot some weeks before. It was similar to the infected foot in the Philippines. A retained wood fragment causes progressive infection, and untreated, loss of limb and

Five loaves and two fishes

even life. I looked at his foot and an amputation was looking likely. So I gave him a shot of ketamine and started work. Villagers gathered. Naturally they had never seen a patient anaesthetised before, and many thought he was dead! I found the wood, dealt with the infection and bandaged him up. He was flat out for 1 hour. But he recovered, and testified to the grace of God, sending the white doctor just in time. As a result of this testimony, many have since been reached through him.

We visited one particular village in January 2007 and again in January 2008. We were in the habit of sending tricky cases to the on looking pastors, so that they could give prayer ministry. On the second visit a woman came to me, carrying a baby. "Do you remember me?" she asked. I had to admit that I did not. So she told me the story. She had attended our clinic 12 months earlier, seeking treatment for infertility. She had been married for some years, with no sign of pregnancy. She thought we might have a medicine for her. I had apparently sent her to the pastors for prayer ministry. And now, a year later, she had a baby! I said how pleased I was. "Doctor, you don't understand" she told me. "This baby was born exactly nine months after that prayer ministry, and is now three months old". Suddenly I realised that God's power works through us, even when we are completely unaware of it. The clinic one year earlier

Five loaves and two fishes

had, no doubt, been busy, and none of us would have picked that lady out as someone to really, really pray for. To labour in prayer for. To call down heaven for. No, we just prayed a simple prayer and she left us. I have seen this many times. It is often in the mundane, when we are faithful to pray, but then get out of God's way, that he does his most exciting works.

But, as we know, life on earth has it's tears and tragedies. Michael had met a beautiful young woman called Gladys. They married in 2006, and he completed his paediatric training in 2008. He had set up a magnificent system which meant that every month he took a team to a rural village, treating sickness and preaching the Gospel. In 2007 Timothy was born, and the family was happy and content. In 2009, Gladys was returning home from work, travelling in a taxi. It was the 6pm rush hour, and Kampala traffic has to be seen to be believed. Somehow the taxi left the road, crashing into a small building. Gladys was knocked unconscious, and was taken to Mulago Hospital, the large teaching hospital in Kampala. She seemed to recover well, but sometime during the night was found collapsed. Desperate attempts were made to resuscitate her, but to no avail. That night Michael lost his lovely wife, and Timothy lost his mummy. Michael never recovered and soon after this he moved away.

Five loaves and two fishes

From that time, Aisha helped us more and more as a Clinical Officer, and we helped Dr Frank to train as a surgeon. As time passed, he and his wife Lydia took over the role Michael had, and our team was functioning once more. Dr Frank and Lydia have become very dear to us, and he is now a well-known surgeon in Kampala. Meanwhile Aisha became not only a key worker, but a close friend. In fact we call her our African daughter, and she calls us Mum and Dad.

Progressively we helped to establish Aisha in a self-funding clinic. The clinic works by providing care to city people who can afford to pay a little for their consultation, the medicines or a pair of reading glasses. From the income, Aisha can earn a small wage, and also have enough to travel and provide rural clinics to the very poor.

As we got to know Aisha, we discovered the remarkable story of her mother's conversion, and subsequently Aisha's. Aisha's Mum is called Faith, and the family background is Muslim. One of Faith's sisters met Christians at school and these Christians had a great influence on her. After some time this sister became a Christian, suffering a good deal of family persecution as a result. She subsequently married a pastor and talked to Faith about the wonderful Jesus she had discovered. Faith did not want to know.

Five loaves and two fishes

Some years later, Faith was married and had children. One night she had a vivid dream. She saw the shape of a building and heard voices singing 'hallelujah.' A voice told her to go and find this place. The next day she was disturbed and perplexed. It was a Sunday, and the more she turned things over in her mind, the more she felt the dream was real. She grappled with her feelings, but eventually she set off down the road, feeling led in one direction. Soon she heard singing, and this amazed her as the words and tune were exactly as in her dream. As she got closer, the shape of the building from where the sound emerged was the building she had seen in her dream! It was a church.

Despite all she had known, her cultural caution, her social reservations and her prior rejection of all things Christian, she felt compelled to enter this building …. this church. She crept in cautiously. Immediately she felt the presence of the One who had known her for all of her life. In one breath she felt drawn, accepted, forgiven and empowered. She fell to her knees in the presence of the Lord of heavens armies. She can't recall how long she spent with her new-found Father, but it was some time. When her tears were dry and she was able to get up from her knees, she resolved to find out all she could of this wonderful heavenly Father.

Five loaves and two fishes

There was nothing that could stop her returning, so she began to visit this fellowship of believers regularly. She got to know Jesus, found forgiveness and new life, and was powerfully drawn to follow Him. She discovered that His presence cleansed her, renewed her, brought her joy, and conveyed life to her. She asked Jesus to fill her, not really understanding that she was becoming a real Christian!

When her husband found out about all of this, he sent her away with her two children. He could only view this as apostasy. Faith had no choice but to return to her village in the east of Uganda. However, her father was a Muslim Imam. He felt disgraced and humiliated by Faith's defection to what he regarded as the "infidel" way of life. He had already seen one daughter go this way, and a second was too painful for him. One night he called the village community together. Faith was asked to choose between her family or her new found Jesus. After all she had discovered, known and appreciated, she chose Jesus and was forced to leave. Her exile from the family was a terribly painful time for her, but it was not to be permanent.

Several months passed before Faith's husband decided to take her back. However he insisted that she did not expose their children to Christian things or take them to church. But Faith could not escape from the joy and

Five loaves and two fishes

knowledge of all she had found. She was in turmoil, and felt her loyalties were in question. After some time Faith felt it would be wrong to exclude her Jesus from her children's lives.

Pastor Emmanuel and his wife Florence pastored the church she had found, and Faith chose to take her children to this lively fellowship whenever her husband was out. Aisha has vivid memories of this part of her childhood. She especially recalls that if her father returned before the family got home on a Sunday, he would turn up at the church and drag them away. Young Aisha watched all that happened. Children are spiritually aware, and very sensitive. They can often detect what is good and right. So it was no surprise that Aisha also found the lovely presence of Jesus, and accepted Him as her saviour. She has never been the same since.

Over time, it is a blessing that Faith's husband, Aisha's father, has softened a little. He accepts that something very real happened to Faith and Aisha, and Aisha is able to talk with him and enjoy a good relationship. Pastor Emmanuel has worked hard to keep on good terms with him also, and a tacit atmosphere of trust developed.

We believe that this true account reminds us that God is always able to gain our attention. If we will not

Five loaves and two fishes

listen when we are awake, he will speak to us in dreams! Let's keep in mind also, that his calling may lead us into a more difficult time, not an easier time.

By the mid 2000's, anti-HIV therapy was just becoming available, thanks to Gordon Brown's negotiations with the world bank over third world debt. He deserves credit in history for saving the lives of millions by insisting that when a nation's debt was cancelled, that nation was mandated to provide anti-HIV therapy. But until then, HIV was rampant in Uganda. Everyone knew of someone who was dying, or had died. The existing orphanages swelled. Families took on dead relatives' children. And here the gospel triumphed. Many churches started schools, orphanages and feeding programmes, the love of Jesus in action.

Many accounts emerged of people being prayed for who had been HIV positive. Some became HIV negative. Thosugh, as doctors, we know that the testing was sometimes not very robust, and some of the claims were spurious, there is no doubt that some were also rigorously tested and very well documented. It is likely that hundreds experienced complete healing from HIV.

Five loaves and two fishes

Chapter 9 - Deeper into Africa - John

During 2005 we had purchased a small bus for Pastor Emmanuel to use for mission. We then used it many times. The roads were so poor that it began to deteriorate quite rapidly. By 2009 it was clear that we needed to buy a better vehicle. So we asked Pastor Emmanuel to keep a look out for a suitable vehicle. It had to transport 12 people, have 4-wheel drive and be robust.

Pastor Emmanuel found a Japanese export which fitted the bill. He told me the price and the details. I received an email from his relative asking that I make the transfer to him. So on a Friday afternoon I visited our local HSBC and activated the transfer of £6,400.

Several days later I received a call from Florence. She told me that their email account had been compromised and to disregard any recent communication. With rising panic I asked about the request to transfer £6,400. She knew nothing of it. We had been cheated. We had no idea how it had happened.

I called the bank in Uganda immediately. The manager said two suspicious individuals were trying to draw money from the account. She told me she would block their access. But then when we subsequently

Five loaves and two fishes

requested the money to be returned to the UK, apparently it could not be found. Pastor Emmanuel could not locate the money. The international fraud department of our bank became involved. But the trail had gone dead. Weeks passed by with no breakthrough. We had recruited praying friends from every continent. The money was from the New Hope charity, much of it given by people who were not well off. Then after twelve weeks I felt God speak very clearly to me. I recall the moment as if it were yesterday. He told me to send £6,400 of our own money to the correct bank, then the original £6,400 would be located and returned to us. Our act of faith was going to release a miracle. I fought with God in prayer! I did not want to risk loosing another large sum. But after a week I gave in. That Monday morning the lady at our bank stared at me with incredulity when I explained, but she carried out the transfer as I had requested. Two days later we received a telephone call from Uganda. The money had been located and was being returned to us! Apparently it had been in the bank manager's private account. Fear of being discovered had resulted in her feeling increasingly guilty and had led her to return it. And so we were able to purchase the bus, which subsequently became known as the 'miracle bus'!

Around this time we started working a little more in the poorer west of the nation, near the Congolese

Five loaves and two fishes

border. Here we met one of Pastor Emmanuel's disciples, a Pastor called Azaria. Let me relate his story as it illustrates the immense difficulty many pastors experience.

In 1983, as a young man, Azaria was forced to seek a job in Kampala. He was not saved, and he stayed in the city doing anything he liked. His life was out of control. Then in 1987 he attended a crusade in Kampala where he met Jesus. From that time, he joined the Pentecostal church where the pastor trained him and helped him to walk with Jesus. He learned how to serve him as the master of life. After two years he felt called into full time ministry.

In 1994 God blessed Azaria with a beautiful wife called Gladys. They started married life with about £2, and were so poor that they could not afford to live, constantly asking themselves where they were going to get money, food and clothes. They had twins and used a banana bud to feed the babies because they could not afford to buy bottles.

The church was very small and there were about 20-30 Christians. He constructed a small grass thatched building where the believers could meet and pray, but as the number of believers was so small they could not manage to support him and Gladys. They rented a small room for about £1 per month, and they could not afford to eat more than once a day. At that stage,

Five loaves and two fishes

the church managed to buy a small piece of land where Azaria constructed a temporary church building. Three years later a strong wind came and hit the church taking away the roof. It was a painful experience. However, over time, brothers and sisters who still supported Azaria helped him to build another church which was a more substantial building.

Over the years, Azaria and Gladys had four more children. In 2005, Gladys became pregnant again. That December she gave birth to a baby girl. But tragedy struck, and shortly after the birth she bled so much that she slowly faded away, and passed into her Father's presence. Azaria was devastated. He thought of leaving the ministry but his friends counseled him to stay. At this stage he was in his 40s, and had 7 children. It was very difficult for him to care for them without a mother. The believers within the church came to his support, and showed him love and care.

The ministry grew, and Azaria began to support another 10 churches in the west of Uganda. The main church in Ishongororo which he started with 25 members grew to over 150, plus over 100 teenagers and children.

Around this time Azaria met Robina. Friendship turned to love and they soon married. She became the new mother of his children. Besides the seven natural

Five loaves and two fishes

children, there were two orphans of Azaria's brother who were living with him. The family now totalled 11, and they lived in a tiny building on a small plot of land. They had only four rooms in which to cook, welcome and sleep. That situation continued for many years.

Meanwhile Azaria and Robina started a school with three classes. They also started a widows' project where they helped many HIV widows. Using a small plot of land they produced food to feed the most needy ones. Somehow God provided for all his children to go to secondary school, which is not provided by the state. Azaria says he could not believe that this could happen. Recently we have been able to build Azaria and Robina a new house, with a concrete base and solid brick walls, and enough space for his extended family.

In 2012 we wanted to help Azaria with transport for his oversight of all the churches. He had been travelling to all the various towns and villages on a bicycle. One Sunday we announced his need to our fellowship. We said he needed £1,000 to buy a motorcycle and have enough left over for servicing and insurance. I made a large photograph of a motorbike and cut it into 100 pieces, selling each piece for £10. I have never seen God's people so captivated! They queued to buy their £10 stake. I

Five loaves and two fishes

sold all the pieces by noon! Having arrived home I received a call. A godly lady wanted to give me the £1,000 in one donation. So we raised £2,000 in a few hours. Azaria got his bike, fuel and servicing for some years, and God's kingdom was advancing.

Meanwhile the medical outreach around Kampala was working well. One weekend the team visited a village where an energetic and visionary pastor led the church. The team treated many sick people, and preached the gospel. However the pastor had thought ahead and knew that people were at their most responsive after such care. So he printed invitations to his Sunday morning service, the next day. What a great move that was. He left the cards on every chair in the clinic. Hundreds picked them up. So the next day many people came to the service. And he preached the gospel clearly. That day dozens responded and accepted Christ, and there were 50 baptisms that same day!

We were in the habit of visiting Kisiizi Hospital in Kabale district, south western Uganda. I would often operate on surgical cases for two weeks while the resident surgeon was able to take a break. On one occasion there was an outbreak of Marburg virus in Kabale district. Marburg is one of a family of viruses, like Ebola which is responsible for viral haemorrhagic fever. That is to say it causes a high temperature and

Five loaves and two fishes

fatal bleeding from multiple sites. The virus is considered to be extremely dangerous with a mortality of around 50%. Myra was working on the medical ward when a man was brought in with a fever early one week. He rapidly deteriorated despite all treatment. By Wednesday he was moribund and at noon on the Thursday he died. Suddenly the staff realised this was probably a case of Marburg. The World Health Organisation (WHO) was called and within hours they arrived in specialised vehicles, isolation suits and using disinfecting sprays. The staff of the ward were advised they might be at risk. At that moment Myra received a text from a good friend who is a prayer partner quoting verses 1-7 from Psalm 91

> *The person who rests in the shadow of the Most High God will be kept safe by the Mighty One. I will say about the Lord, "He is my place of safety. He is like a fort to me. He is my God. I trust in him." He will certainly save you from hidden traps and from deadly sickness. He will cover you with his wings. Under the feathers of his wings you will find safety. He is faithful. He will keep you safe like a shield or a tower. You won't have to be afraid of the terrors that come during the night. You won't have to fear the arrows that come at you during the day. You won't have to be afraid of the sickness that attacks in the darkness. You won't have to fear the plague that destroys at noon. A thousand*

Five loaves and two fishes

may fall dead at your side. Ten thousand may fall near your right hand. But no harm will come to you.

We knew immediately that God was speaking and that all would be well. A total of 18 people in the area had contracted Marburg in the weeks before our visit, and 9 had died. But neither Myra nor any of the staff became ill and we returned home unscathed. People often ask us if we are worried in such settings, or when there is war or violence. Our answer is that if we are called, and in his service, we are under his protection.

Five loaves and two fishes

Chapter 10 - Francophone Africa at last - Myra

We have always loved France and the French language. Back in the 1990 we felt that Jesus laid on our hearts a desire to work in Francophone Africa. Initially we thought that would happen immediately. But in due course we learnt that God's call prepares us, it does not propel us! In fact sometimes it seems that our dreams take a long time to come to fruition.

We were, therefore, very excited to receive an email from a doctor who had worked for John in Leeds. She had been an outstanding junior colleague, a believer and a lovely person to work with. During her medical student elective in Gabon she met an eye technician called Henri. An eye technician is a person trained in eye surgery but without a medical degree.

When they met, Henri spoke no English and Joyce very little French. They only met each other a few days before she went home but she says she knew even then that he would one day be her husband. They started writing to each other, communicating by using bible verses that each could read in their own language! But love found a way, and they learned French and English as their language of love. They had to overcome many obstacles and family concern before they married but they are a truly wonderful team. Joyce has passion and drive to make things

Five loaves and two fishes

happen and Henri has a relaxed easygoing persistence. Joyce is very type A while Henri is horizontally laid back with a solid faith and a truly servant heart. Their spunky children are also a fantastic part of their family ministry to the poor and needy.

Together they had moved to the old French Congo now known as the Congo Republic, or Congo Brazzaville, as distinct from the old Zaire or the Belgian Congo which is now known as the Democratic Republic of Congo. They were working in a very remote small hospital in the north where they had developed an eye surgery charity for those who could not afford the usual costs of such treatment. It is a great joy to see the before and after pictures of Henri's sight-restoring operations.

Joyce told us that they were running into a medical staffing crisis and asked us if we could offer any time to help fill the gaps. We were very keen to go and as we prayed it felt right. Since we had already retired we could offer six weeks. So we flew to Brazzaville just after New Year and stayed a night in the local guesthouse linked to the hospital. We were expecting to fly north the following morning but found there were no commercial flights running! These things tend to happen in this part of the world with no explanation. Joyce thought we would be able to get one of the UNHCR (United Nations High Commission

Five loaves and two fishes

for Refugees) flights which flew twice a week to the hospital due north in Impfondo. The town is not easily accessible by road because of the swampland and forest, and the only alternative is by river in a floating antique which takes a week or two!

We arrived at the airport 3 days later with tickets for the UN flight. Our bags and our bodies were weighed and we sat in the departure lounge for nearly an hour only to be told that two personnel from Medicines sans Frontiers had arrived and had taken priority. So we returned to the guesthouse, waiting for the next flight a few days later. Meanwhile our extra suitcases and all the equipment we had brought for Joyce was loaded onto the ancient barges to be transported north by river. This was the last convoy as the rainy season was over and the river would soon be too dry for further convoys.

We were very dismayed at first but then accepted the fact that our Heavenly Father had grounded us for a bit of R and R! We spent time reading and praying and looking around Brazzaville. The city has the air of faded glory, it's once grand buildings crumbling and decrepit. The riverside boulevard looked decidedly disheveled. Clearly three decades of communism and a decade of civil war had taken their toll. Happily there had been stability for the last 10 years.

Five loaves and two fishes

Later that week with a sense of déjà vu, we returned to the airport and had the usual weigh-in before proceeding to departures. There we were accosted by an employee who informed us that a sick man was being flown back from Impfondo and 2 seats had been removed to make way for the stretcher so only one of us could fly. So we had to switch a few things in our bags and I had to leave John behind in Brazzaville. Ironically if John had been able to fly north he could have treated the man's fractured pelvis and saved him a journey!

After about an hour in this 12 seater plane we landed and we were all ushered off. Some people were collecting their bags and it was not clear whether or not we had reached our destination but a brusque woman speaking in unclear French shoved a plastic card in my hand and ordered me into a hut where we waited. It seemed that this was a stopover and we were in fact across the border in DRC. There were also a couple of fighter planes on the tarmac which didn't feel very reassuring! Eventually what felt like a remnant was herded back on the plane and we were all required to hand in our plastic card which clearly formed some sort of airport security.

I was glad to reach Impfondo, and I was met by a delightful missionary from the hospital who had lived

Five loaves and two fishes

there several decades. She spoke not only fluent French but several tribal languages as well.

The hospital was in an old communist training camp which had been given to a Christian charity when the communist regime ended. I was accommodated in a small wooden hut at the far end of the compound and shared kitchen facilities with a young man from the USA who was Mr Fix-it. His main role seemed to be keeping the hospital supplied with electricity and since the generator had died they were powering everything from an old tractor!

I started work in the outpatients and my French took a very steep learning curve upwards as there was no one to translate from English. In addition a lot of the tribal people only spoke Lingala so one of the reception staff had to help translating my French into the tribal tongue and back again. Somehow we managed and all the patients were seen. The ward round had been similarly taxing and I was very tired by the end of the day.

Sleeping wasn't easy as there was not enough electricity for fans even if they had existed and my bedroom was around 30 degrees and felt airless. It had a tiny window to the outside where the temperature was not much lower.

Five loaves and two fishes

Joyce and Henri had been very smart and shipped solar panels for the roof of their small home. This meant they could run a fridge and occasional air conditioning! So it was a joy to be in their lovely cool room when I went across for meals. They have three delightful children who kept me entertained and loved having visitors. Henri had grown up in a very poor village but when his father went blind he vowed he would do something to save others from devastating loss of vision.

After setting up an eye clinic in Gabon, which became self-sustaining, they were led to move to Congo Brazzaville. It has been an uphill battle because of the remote situation and unbelievable bureaucracy. They had submitted a nineteen page document to be able to transport the operating microscope into the country and then it had to make the precarious upstream journey on rotting barges which had also brought our suitcases. They had just installed it the week we arrived and we were privileged to see the bandages removed from their first two patients who whooped for joy because they could see again. Since our visit they have gone from strength to strength raising thousands of pounds for the clinic and getting international recognition for their pioneering work.

John, meanwhile, was kicking his heels in Brazzaville. He had become the best customer in the local coffee

Five loaves and two fishes

shop which had free internet. He was nearly on first name terms with the local taxi drivers! At last after 10 days in the capital he finally got on the UN flight, but he knew throughout that God had his plans.

It was good to be together again and when he arrived I spent the afternoon showing him the ropes in outpatients. We were told we would be on-call that night which was a little daunting.

Our accommodation was a good walk from the emergency room across a dark, insect infested field, but at least twice that night we had to make the trek as understanding the admission nurses speaking fast, African-accented French on a crackling mobile phone was very challenging. So a face-to-face encounter was the only way forward! We shone our torches in all directions as we walked hoping to rouse any sleepy snakes before we trod on them. The expeditions were, however, a welcome respite from the stuffy heat of our small bedroom.

The next day started badly when there were no matches for the kerosene stove. Our kind Congolese neighbours lent us some but then the kerosene ran out so it was lukewarm coffee and dry bread for breakfast but we reminded ourselves that this was more than some of the locals would have that day so we didn't grumble much! The morning ward round took three

Five loaves and two fishes

hours and there were so many patients waiting for the clinic by the time we had finished that the queue wasn't cleared till late afternoon. By then we were very tired. A weekend on-call was looming so we were eager to get some rest before our services were needed again.

The doctor we had come to relieve had already left and alongside the female obstetrics doctor we were the only medics.

The patients at Impfondo were really sick. Many of them don't seek medical attention until very late and some are sent to the Christian hospital from the local government hospital. The later group have often had quite inadequate or inappropriate treatment so are at death's door and often beyond help when they are admitted. A large number of patients are HIV positive with associated infections such as tuberculosis. There is a dedicated clinic in the hospital run by a specialist nurse who monitors the treatment regimes and tries to encourage compliance with the tablets. The free supply by the World Health Organisation (WHO) and others has made such a difference to the treatment of HIV and related problems in sub-saharan Africa but the medication does have unpleasant side effects and without proper understanding many patients do default and die of complications.

Five loaves and two fishes

There was a good deal of child malnutrition particularly among the indigenous Pygmy tribes which are often exploited and enslaved by their Bantu neighbours who migrated in earlier centuries from north Africa.

Each day started at 7am with 30 minutes of prayer with all the hospital staff followed by a bible talk. We could usually follow when it was in French but sometimes it was in Lingala so we were completely lost. John operated on the surgical cases. Many were in the advanced stages of disease. When it was an emergency in the middle of the night we had to wake the friendly American DIY man to crank up the tractor and power the electricity in theatre!

We were pleasantly surprised to get a message that our luggage sent by barge from Brazzaville had eventually arrived in the port. As I was finished in clinic I was able to go down to the river to see it unloaded. Looking at the barges which disgorged the loads from their deep holds it was hard to believe they actually floated and I was glad we didn't have to make the journey our bags had made. Teams of men worked to unpack the contents of every shape and purpose. Meanwhile a mother cooked fish on the wooden deck with a kerosene stove while her baby played nearby. No health and safety rules applied in this place.

Five loaves and two fishes

In the midst of our busy days we were pre-warned to be ready for a Skype call on January 21st which is our daughter's birthday. Her brother, James, was in the know about an imminent proposal of marriage and wanted us ready to celebrate the news. The call duly arrived late in the evening after Becci had been literally led up the garden path in James and Hannah's Liverpool garden, blindfolded to where Elikem had created a truly romantic setting in which to "pop the question". As they sipped champagne together in the UK we toasted them online with our lukewarm water. Of course there would be further champagne celebrating on our return.

The days continued to be busy with clinics and operating. On our second weekend we were privileged to be taken to an Aka (Pygmy) village and a nearby church service. We didn't understand a word but the congregation was very welcoming. After the service we walked a couple of miles to another village and had a tour of the forest with explanations from our guide about the medicinal qualities of various plants. Apparently there were at least three remedies for piles!

The Aka people are really poor. They live in a sort of feudal system with the dominant Bantu tribe. They are supposed to bring any game they catch in the forest for their Bantu masters but they often hide it in the forest

Five loaves and two fishes

and pretend they have caught nothing so they can eat it later.

The Canadian missionary from the hospital works with them and the many leprosy sufferers who no longer have active disease but live with the consequences of destruction to nerves, joints and skin resulting from the infection. She had been in Impfondo for many years and communicated freely with the local tribal people.

Soon after the lovely news of Becci's engagement we received the very sad news that our dear friend and neighbour had rapidly deteriorated and died. The cancer he had fought so stoically finally caught up with him. We had become very close during our years in Heswall. We had shared ownership of a boat in Conway and undertaken many sailing trips together. We were devastated that we were not around to support him and his wife in his final days. We were also sure that in view of the struggle getting an internal flight to Impfondo it would be almost impossible to return early for his funeral. We went through several days with heavy hearts.

Around that time were un-expectantly joined by an experienced doctor from the USA and two medical students. They found their feet after a few days and began to get more involved in day to day work. As I was praying early one morning I got a deep sense that

Five loaves and two fishes

as reinforcements had arrived we were no longer indispensable and we should try to return for the funeral. We grappled with the pull of responsibility versus relationship. Eventually we decided that in 10 years we would have wished for only one thing; - that we had gone back. When I rang another friend and neighbour to check the date and say we were thinking of coming home she told me that when Freddie was dying he had asked for John to speak at his funeral. That settled it and we decided to find a way to be there.

Air France staff were not helpful on the phone and said they normally only allowed flight changes for close relatives. The cost of new tickets at short notice was apparently over £3,000! We decided we would get to Brazzaville as step number one, and then work out the flight to UK.

As on the way to Impfondo the seats on UNHCR flights were precious so we requested prayer from all our friends so we could get the Thursday flight. We bought our tickets and went to the airport with Joyce, Henri and family. We made it onto the flight and heard later that several charity workers had not made it. We watched as the lovely Samoutou family waved from the airstrip growing smaller and smaller as we rose into the air.

Five loaves and two fishes

The journey was quite long because we made a detour north to pick up charity workers from a remote village with just a mud runway. Later we stopped on the far side of the Congo river in the DRC to refuel. Finally we arrived in Brazzaville after 4:30pm.

We went directly from the airport to the Air France office in town only to reach there as they locked their doors for the day! It was Thursday evening and Air France only flew three times a week. We needed seats on the Friday night flight in order to get home for the Monday funeral. The hope of changing our flights was kept beyond our reach. So early Friday morning we were the first at the Air France office as it opened.

We duly took a queuing number – even though there was no one else waiting! Our hearts sank when we were directed to the most grumpy-looking all the desk clerks. She kept yawning and clearly had experienced a bad night. We explained the situation and sat in silence as she checked our tickets and then gave us the answer. 'C'est pas possible' she said, which means 'it's not possible'. She rotated her computer screen to show us the large text "no change, no refund". She said we would have to buy new tickets and we knew from the website that the current price for the weekend was £1,200 each just to get as far as Paris. To be fair, our tickets were the cheapest internet ones we could

Five loaves and two fishes

find when we bought them, and we had done our research – this class was not changeable or refundable.

We pleaded the closeness of our relationship with Freddie and asked to talk to the director. With lack of conviction she agreed that she would talk to him. She was gone for a long time and we prayed fervently. There is a verse in Proverbs which says "the king's heart is a stream of water in the hands of the Lord and He turns it where He wills." We prayed that the director's heart would be so.

She came back and asked for the death certificate and GP letter. Our GP friend Sophie had kindly emailed a supportive letter outlining the closeness of our relationship to the family. She returned asking us to translate the letter into French, apparently trusting what we said. When she returned again she still had a solemn face and told us off for not reading the small print stating the non-refundable and non-changeable nature of our tickets. Then she refunded them, charged us a small fee and re-issued fresh tickets!! We were ready to fly at 22:50pm that night! We were both close to tears and we left the bureau walking on air. It was another mission miracle!

We realised that had we arrived before they closed the previous night the staff would have been eager to leave and the director would probably already have

Five loaves and two fishes

gone so God's last minute timing was perfect as always.

Five loaves and two fishes

Chapter 11 - We never imagined this! - John

In 2012 Myra and I met Pastor Alexandre, who works in the Democratic Republic of Congo, or DRC. He was visiting Liverpool at the invitation of Frontline Church. By this stage James was project lead for the church's 'Love Congo' project and had been to the DRC earlier in the year.

Pastor Alexandre had given up a well-paid job as a banker to serve as a pastor. He was based in Butembo, in the dangerous rebel-smitten land in eastern DRC. This massive ex-Belgian colony is distinct from the ex-French Republic of Congo, previously visited. In particular, it is much poorer, and has been war-torn for many years with around 6 million civilians losing their lives as a result. Though being two thirds the size of Western Europe, and possessing much mineral wealth, at the time of writing it is ranked by the IMF as being one of the world's three poorest nations, with an average annual income of $394 for each citizen. Through the many journeys God has taken us on, he seems to have led us to this francophone African nation, and we see it as our main overseas mission focus for the years we have remaining.

In 2013 Frontline Church ran a mission to the city of Butembo. The poverty was beyond anything I had seen. Having travelled to over 50 nations, at least 30

Five loaves and two fishes

being resource-poor, I thought I had witnessed extreme poverty. But here the people had virtually nothing. No running water, no electricity, no roads or drains, no postal service and no free schooling. Of course the capital Kinshasa, like all the world's capital cities, has experienced investment. There are high rise buildings that powerful lights play over at night. There are tarmac roads and intermittent mains electricity. But within 10 miles of the city limits that all stops, and the landscape is bleakly adorned with deeply rutted mud roads, wobbly shacks and grass huts.

We travelled overland from Uganda, leaving western Uganda near Kasese at a designated border crossing into the Congolese town of Kasindi. From there we drove on mud tracks for 6 hours to Butembo. The journey rattles every one of the 208 bones in the body. It involves traversing a dangerous corridor on the eastern side of the DRC which runs from Beni in the north to Goma in the south, very close to the Rwanda border. This north-south corridor is home to many warring factions, and vicious attacks on the indigenous villagers are common. Whole communities are wiped out. Sometimes just the men are killed. The purpose, besides taking land and possessions, is to instill fear and terror among the people. The perpetrators are rarely caught as they look like everyone else. As a consequence, travel is dangerous for the hours it takes to cross the area, and there are many thousands of

Five loaves and two fishes

displaced people from the area who flee as far as they can. Rwanda will not take them in, refusing to offer asylum, and Uganda have taken a limited number, so many have become "internally displaced peoples" (IDPs). Most have fled to the safety of Kasindi where rebels seem unwilling to attack, perhaps due to it's proximity to the Uganda border.

In Butembo we spent a number of days teaching and training pastors and church members in outreach. As we were making our way back to Uganda, and while still within the dangerous corridor, our ancient vehicle began to overheat. We were near a river, and the driver wanted us to clamber down the bank and fill some containers he had. Forest was on either side, and I sensed danger. I knew that a vehicle could appear from the dense foliage ahead, and one behind, trapping us. What could follow did not bear consideration. I asked everyone to sacrifice their drinking water and top up the hot radiator as quickly as possible from their bottles. So we were back in motion within a few minutes. Two hours later we reached the border, and shortly after we learned that a bus following us had been held up by rebels at the exact place where we had stopped. Everyone had been taken off, stripped and robbed, though fortunately no one had been injured. The Lord of heaven's armies had been in that place with us. No

Five loaves and two fishes

doubt the rebels had been there also, and must have seen us stop.

In the border town of Kasindi, we quickly realised that this was a strategic opportunity, as we could easily get there, it was relatedly safe, and it contained many very needy people. God was to confirm this to us the following year, but already our thoughts were on establishing an evangelistic health centre in the village.

A return trip to the DRC in October 2014 was a little overshadowed by the Ebola outbreak raging in West Africa. I had planned to go via Ghana for an orthopaedic training course but had to abort this as all travel in and out of Ghana was being strictly controlled. When my flight was cancelled I decided to go early to Uganda ahead of the rest of the team and get all the necessary purchases of medicines, solar panels etc.

Meanwhile Myra followed with nurse Tracey. At check-in one of their cases was overweight. Normally we are very careful but the weekend had been a bit fraught and so packing wasn't done so well. Tracey had a lot of space in her hand luggage so they threw a pile of things into it and that case and checked-in without problem.

Five loaves and two fishes

They had not really considered that what they had transferred were bags and bags of tablets pre-packed for the clinics in small plastic packets. As they went through security Tracey's case was pulled aside as it failed the x-ray screening. The security man started to empty the case, pulling out dozens of little packets of tablets to the horror and amazement of other passengers. Myra and Tracey imagined themselves about to be detained, arrested and interrogated by the drugs squad. They saw themselves in court the next day, the trip finished before it had started. However, with a flourish the security man pulled out an old manual sphygmomanometer (blood pressure machine) and declared that this was the problem. They laughed with relief and happily demonstrated it's function to measure blood pressure! It seemed that he was blind to the tablets, not even mentioning them! Our angels were working overtime, but we sensed they laughed with us that day!

We met in Kampala and our journey west was uneventful. The miracle minibus drove us the 6 hours to Mbarara, then ultimately via Kasese across the border into the Democratic Republic of Congo. This was to be a scoping visit to assess the viability of building the clinic in Kasindi. We had not intended to do any hands-on work but use the 24 hours to talk, discuss and plan. Unfortunately there had been a misunderstanding and 100 patients were sitting outside

Five loaves and two fishes

the mud hut which was the temporary clinic. We managed with some shared equipment, a few medicines and a handful of impromptu translators. We were very impressed by the nurse running the clinic who turned out to be Pastor Alexandre's daughter!

We met all the local dignitaries who clearly wanted to know our intentions and motives but seemed satisfied with our responses. They were also keen to get free medical advice and we felt we had made good connections for the future. The head of the border police brought his family for help, their daughter had a complex kidney problem.

Our impressions of the location were very positive as the town felt very safe but has clearly been the place of refuge for many people fleeing violence in nearby areas so there was a great need for medical care.

That same night as Myra was falling asleep she had an experience like nothing she experienced before. She spoke of watching what can only be described as a vision. She saw many tortured and anguished black faces and then felt carried along with them on a fast flowing river. The whole episode lasted about 10 minutes and she struggled to sleep, praying to try and make sense of what she had seen. It was 12 months later when we began to understand what God had been saying.

Five loaves and two fishes

The following morning we were welcomed at the church, where we spoke, and after a hurried lunch headed for the border to get through before it closed. Unlike our immigration the day before we were speeded through the process by our newly found friend at the border control whose daughter we had examined the night before!

In October 2015 whilst returning from a trip to Kasindi we spent some time chatting with the border officials who were all struggling to read as they had reached the age where your arms are not long enough to hold the paper far enough away. We had in our possession a few pairs of £1 reading glasses and fitted each person with an appropriate strength pair. We departed with much smiling and shaking of hands and headed to the Uganda crossing.

Most of our team paid their re-entry visa fee but we had no need of a visa because we possessed Irish passports which allow free passage. Unfortunately our Congo visa was in our English passports and therefore no exit stamp appeared in our Irish ones. The Ugandan official got very obstructive and started accusing us of knowingly breaking the law. We suspected he was looking for a bribe and saw that we were not going to be allowed in. It was getting close to dusk when the border closed so we had to act quickly. We hailed a

Five loaves and two fishes

motorbike taxi and headed back across the river for the half mile journey to Congo. We were greeted with delight by the policeman on the gate who had been treated in our clinic the day before and once inside the office we were met with open arms by the border clerks. They made some disparaging remarks about the Ugandans and happily put an exit stamp in our Irish passports. We jumped back onto the motorbike and raced back to Uganda where we got through just before the border closed for the night.

We have experienced a lot of border mini-miracles! The first was getting to Norway all those years ago without passports. Myra had another in April 2015 when visiting Becci, who had moved Ghana. She was so excited about the trip but there was a niggle in her spirit and when she waited at the check in longer than usual it grew. "Did you know your visa is expired, madam?" Everyone looked at her passport but finally all agreed she couldn't travel. They were extremely kind and booked her on the flight the next day but she still had to get a visa that has a 24 hour turnaround even in emergencies. She took the first flight to London and started the online application, booking an appointment at the Ghana High Commission. The only one she could book was 9.30hrs the next day but the flight was at 13.20hrs. The Ghana High Commission was virtually on the other side of London, and many miles from Heathrow Airport.

Five loaves and two fishes

She rang and was told she could turn up today without an appointment, but all the papers had to be printed. Somehow she got into the BA business lounge and struggled with the technology, but managed finally to print everything by 11.45hrs. She got the Heathrow express to Paddington, grabbed some not too bad passport photographs in the booth in the foyer and ran for a taxi whilst calling the Ghana High Commission to confirm she was on the way.

She knew she couldn't make High Commission before they closed at 13.00hrs, so she rang to say she couldn't make it. A lovely girl said she would wait for her till 13.30hrs. Myra then got a mobile call from the angel at the High Commission to tell her to phone her on her mobile at the gate and she would be let in. She finally arrived at 1.45pm. By 2.30pm she had a visa in her hand! She told helpful staff member everyone had been praying. The lady smiled and said "We pray that we know who are the genuine people needing help" Myra could have kissed her!

Later in 2015 we were back in DRC. We had made a plan to buy some land for our "New Hope Clinic", but when we arrived the local medical officer, who needs to approve such things, helpfully advised us to look for another, larger plot. It so happened that the land-owner selling the small plot had a larger one nearby,

Five loaves and two fishes

and for a small sum (by western standards) we purchased a plot of land of 2,000 square metres!

We asked if we could meet the internally displaced people (IDPs) and one of Pastor Alexandre's friends, Pastor Dan, who works in Kasindi, called the man who acted as their leader. His name was Adolf and, together with many of the IDPs he had been in Kasindi for years, being taken in by the locals. It was a case of the extremely poor looking after the completely destitute. The majority were women, many of whom had witnessed the savage murder of their own sons, husbands and fathers.

We invited the poorest 100 to the church, and prepared gifts of clothing, rice, salt and soap. We spoke to them about Jesus and the love he has for them. As we stood before them, Myra suddenly realised these were the faces she had seen in her dream the year before. She was overwhelmed by the experience, but knew at once that God had drawn us to this place, and that we had work to do.

Now two years later the health centre is on the brink of completion. During our visit in 2016 we had poured over the plans with Pastor Alexandre, nurse Glorieuse and other wise heads. We had small squares of paper to scale on the plan of our plot. These were shuffled and reshuffled till the local team members were happy

Five loaves and two fishes

with a configuration that would work. This was then passed to the engineer for proper drawings. Two days later we had very professional drawings showing a rather aspirational two way road and roundabout adjacent to the clinic! As we stood on the land there was barely a walking track from the nearby dirt road.

We have been operating a feeding program from the churches for the most malnourished of the IDP children. These skinny little ones have all gained weight but this is an emergency activity and in the longer term we want to start farming initiatives to help their parents support their own families.

Twelve months ago, distressed by the number of displaced children hanging around the streets, we enquired if there were any teachers among the displaced adults. In DRC there is no free education, even at primary school level. We discovered there were four and prevailed upon Pastor Dan to open his church building in the week so they could get some schooling. So the temporary education began and was shared among three churches in the town.

Six months later we were told they had built wooden classrooms and started to follow the national curriculum with four teachers in full time employment. We were thrilled by their initiative and happy to help with funds. This was such a delight to us because we no longer want to be the great white man benefactors but to collaborate with our partners on the ground and

Five loaves and two fishes

see them leading out with their own initiatives. Self-sustainability and empowerment of locals, as mentioned previously, has always been our goal.

Very recently we had another border experience. Our team consisted of James, our doctor friend Doug, Myra and I. We were in Uganda, meeting Pastor Emmanuel, Dr Frank and his wife Nurse Lydia, then we moved west to Ishangororo. We met there with Pastor Azarius and other school leaders. Pastor Emmanuel's daughter, Nora, an educationalist came with us to ensure the school was able to meet increasingly stringent criteria. Then we moved on to the DRC border to see the emerging clinic building and do various pieces of training.

However, before we left the UK, despite applying for our DRC visas over two months earlier, they were not ready, and we had to ask for our passports back and fly without them. This is highly unusual - visas for the DRC usually arrive around one month after application. And travelling without them does not mean they can be purchased at the border. In fact we know this is rarely permitted. But we had no choice.

We approached the border with faith, unsure what would happen, but sensing God had a plan. We were interviewed by the Head of the Immigration Department. He spoke with us in a kindly manner, took all our details, then asked us to wait outside. He planned to call the office in Goma where the Kivu area

Five loaves and two fishes

headquarters are based, as we were in North Kivu District.

Meanwhile we met a number of people at the 'no-man's land' border office. Nora, a Ugandan lady who speaks English and many local languages including Lugandan and Swahili, and who has translated for us previously, came first. We embraced, we shared news and she waited for us.

Dr Guy, a local doctor who supports Glorieuse came next and we agreed on some training needs that Doug and I could deliver.

Then Adolf, the refugee leader brought one of his people. He was a polio victim, unable to walk, but in his village he had learned to earn a living as a cobbler. Then the rebels came and he was carried to safety, but left behind his 'tricycle' contraption that he sat on and pedalled with his hands. He also left behind all his tools. Since fleeing to the safety of Kasindi he had shuffled on his bottom, and, having no tools, could no longer earn any money.

We had remembered him, and had bought a second-hand wheel chair in the UK, which we brought out. Then, while in Kampala we had asked a street-side cobbler to take us to a supplier of cobbler's tools. Deep in the teaming underground market I found a man selling cobbler's knives, chisels, awls, lasts, threads, glue and other bits and pieces. I filled a box.

Five loaves and two fishes

So when we met we gave him the wheel chair. His face lit up and he was so delighted! Then we gave him the box of cobbler's tools. He looked as if Christmas had come! He was so happy that passers-by stopped and took pictures of him.

But then we heard the news. The Head of Immigration called us back to his office. He spoke to us with a sad tone, "C'est pas bon, Vous n'avez pas les visas" *"Its not good. You don't have visas"*

I felt a bit numb. We had come all this way, having already bought land and having started building. Our intentions were purely to benefit Congolese people. And we had plans to deliver teaching in several areas.

We prayed and thought. We were given a possibility of applying again by email direct to Kinshasha, the capital, but it was very costly. So we opted to put James forward for this, and the email and payment were duly made. Then we crossed back into Uganda feeling quite wrung out. What was God doing? We had seen border miracles several times. We could not understand, but remained trusting.

James waited, and the other three of us arranged for key people to join us in our hotel which was a short walk from the DRC border.

So the following day Myra taught Nora to make 'Mwezi pads', which many women at home had cut

Five loaves and two fishes

out, and which are rapidly sewn together to make reusable menstrual pads. Many girls in Africa avoid school when having a period, and many women will not leave their homes. The pads therefore give freedom to many. In fact we brought 100 in kit form, but we hope that the skill will propagate.

In the process of teaching, we learned that Nora had been a Muslim, and had become a Christian 14 years earlier having been prayed for when she was ill with (what we believe was) a duodenal ulcer. The day a pastor prayed for her was the day she was healed. Her family ejected her from the family home, and they wanted to kill her. So she lived in the church for 3 years until her father asked her to return. He, and several other family members subsequently came to Christ. So we recorded a video of Nora's testimony. Then Myra shared with her all the things that were on her heart which she would have taught to the DRC women. Nora promised to faithfully convey this, and in these exchanges, Myra and Nora became very close. Aisha, in Kampala, is our first African daughter. Nora became our second that day.

On the same day, Doug taught two local Congolese doctors, Dr Guy and Dr Paul in a French language approach to children's illness. The two of them are supporting our emerging clinic. He taught them a system which ensures that the symptoms are matched with the likely diagnoses, with questions that eliminate

Five loaves and two fishes

the diagnoses that do not fit. Quickly, the most likely diagnosis is found.

The next day I ran an ultrasound training session for them both, teaching ultrasound physics and showing them various scanning techniques which they had not previously learned. It was a joy, teaching all day in French. Though I have taught this material many times, it was the first time I had done this in French. And Drs Guy and Paul brought 6 pregnant ladies across the border from DRC! The purpose was for me to do dating scans, and allow the two trainees to see vital organs.

Myra recorded a video message for the internally displaced people (IDP) - ie the refugees, on the iPad we had given Pastor Dan last year. She could not meet them, but she could speak, and show them her love.

Meanwhile James waited with a packed bag. He spent time with Pastors Dan and Alexandre. He helped with the training which the rest of the team delivered. But his visa never arrived. And so after we had done all we could, we realised that on this occasion we were not to see any border miracles.

I can't explain this, except that Father God knows best, and seeking God's will in prayer is not like seeking money from an ATM machine. Prayer is an interactive exchange with another living being, our heavenly

Five loaves and two fishes

Father. And our Father knows all things, and always acts for our good. So as we reflected, the cobbler was helped as we planned. The Mwezi pads would be made. Myra spoke to the IDPs by video. We recorded Nora's amazing testimony, and Nora would convey Myra's teaching to the women.

More than that, Nora found a Mum, and Myra found another daughter. Doug and John forged a special bond with the two doctors. And on the Sunday morning we left, the team preached in two separate churches, forming more special bonds. Then Pastor Alexandre showed us a video of the new clinic building, now nearing roof-height.

We have to conclude that God has His plans which often we cannot see. But we also concluded that we had achieved all we had set out to do. Its just that we did not set foot in DRC. We were just a few metres away.

Five loaves and two fishes

Chapter 12 - The God of miracles - John

In Mat 17:20-21 Jesus spoke to his disciples saying, "Your faith is much too small. What I'm about to tell you is true. If you have faith as small as a mustard seed, it is enough. You can say to this mountain, 'Move from here to there.' And it will move. Nothing will be impossible for you."

The reference to moving a mountain is typically Jewish - exaggeration to make a point. And the point is that we all have mountains in our lives - a character flaw that constantly hinders us, an awful work situation, a heart breaking family, a physical illness, a financial burden that seems insurmountable. We can easily think that our problem is the worst. As always, Jesus is tackling the nitty gritty issues of life.

Everest at 29,000 ft is said to be the highest mountain on earth. Hundreds have died on the mountain. But in fact the highest mountain on earth is actually Mount Kea in Hawai - 33,000 ft from it's base to it's summit. It is not well known however, simply because it's base is at the bottom of the ocean. Less than half is visible above the water and no one freezes to death on it, or falls off it.

How is this relevant? Well Jesus says that with faith a mountain can move into the sea. The mountain in the

Five loaves and two fishes

sea is still there! But when it has moved it's not the same problem. Jesus is saying that the relationship we have with our mountain can shift.

We can begin to see how this works when we see in scripture that when the going gets tough, the tough look to God. Think about the spies in the book of Numbers, The Twelve Spies were a group of Israelite chieftains, one from each of the Twelve Tribes, who were dispatched by Moses to scout out the Land of Canaan for 40 days during the time the Israelites were in the desert. The account is found in Numbers 13:1-14:9.

They all saw the enormous task. They all saw the opposition. They all knew it was virtually impossible. But only 2 of them saw God and his plan, and knew his ability to do what he says. So only 2 came back saying it was possible.

So we can see that when we encounter a mountain in our lives we need to look at Him, not at the problem. Focus on God. That's why worship is so vital. In worship we can enter his presence. And it is life transforming. It brings revelation, cleansing, inspiration and inner transformation. That's also why we need to get into His Word. It shows us God's ways, and suddenly we see that they are very different from our own ways. As a result the relationship we

Five loaves and two fishes

have with our mountain can shift. It may still be there, but like Mount Kea compared with Mount Everest.

There is something else. As we have observed, God is not an ATM machine. We can't get a PIN code and get the goods. And yet we sometimes want to treat him in that way. The fact is that as children with a heavenly Father we have a relationship with him, and the more we get to know him, the more we will know how he will react when we are faced with a crisis. Like Mary at the wedding in Cana. She knew that Jesus would step in when the wine ran out. And, incidentally, this shows us how he is interested in the practical, mundane "unspiritual" aspects of life.

Myra and I increasingly predict what the other is thinking. We finish sentences for each other, and know what comment each will make in a certain situation. How? By walking together a long time. And it is the same when we walk with God for a while. We stop looking for ATM PIN code solutions, and begin to sense his heart in a given situation. Which might be different from the last situation.

I am so grateful that Jesus healed blind people differently each time. Otherwise we would have Bible Colleges all around the world devoted to emulating what he did! But there is no formula. Its a relationship.

Five loaves and two fishes

There is one more principle in turning Mount Everest into Mount Kea. Its all to do with how far our believing takes us. In western circles we love to talk about things, such as what we believe about a certain matter, and what that truth means. And all that's great. But as disciples we are supposed to be learners. That's what the Greek word for disciple means - 'mathetes'. Now educationalists agree that learning has several vital bits. One is appreciating truth. The second is being apprenticed to do it. And the third is being fully immersed in doing it without help. When we learned French we sat in a classroom and learned words and grammar. But it was only when we spoke with French people that we moved forward as apprentices. Eventually we began to speak French freely, only when we spent weeks and weeks immersed in a completely French environment.

What am I saying? Western believers tend to live their Christian lives by hearing lots, and maybe by reading lots, but often devoid of much _doing_. Devoid of being apprenticed by others that _do_. Actually devoid of risk. And we wonder why we feel the need for our souls to be jump-started or our spirits resuscitating. We can't break free by hearing even more stuff. That's like simply pulling on our bootlaces. We break free by taking on risk beyond our comfort zone.

Five loaves and two fishes

Scripture is full of weak people who found this out. Consider Joseph, Gideon, David, Esther and Peter. Joseph soon learned that God is bigger than any circumstance he could find himself in. Gideon was a coward when an angel appeared and called him 'mighty warrior'! Suddenly another power was on the case. So he took the risk and saw the nation saved. David had just been anointed and believed God had something for him. But he did not know what. Suddenly an intensely important and critical situation arose. He must have asked himself "Was this what I was anointed for?" And he got involved, risking all. And the nation was saved. Esther was the same. She was moved around like a pawn in a chess game. She had no choices. These days she could have filed a legal case about abuse and exploitation. But her question was similar. "Is this why I am here?" She took the risk and saved the nation. Peter was a feint-hearted fisherman who denied Jesus and then discovered his calling and became a church father.

Risk is the connection between all we believe and all we can be. When we go on mission, people often say we must have strong faith. But we don't. All we have is just enough faith to go, a belief that God could use our puny offerings, and a desire to make a difference. Sometimes that results in finding we are in risky situations. And at those times our faith suddenly grows! We have seen many people come with us who

Five loaves and two fishes

suddenly become faith giants when they did the same. We discover that our heavenly Father is right with us when we do not expect him to be there.

One of those friends we took with us on an early mission to South America ended up working in an Islamic nation. She faced opposition, and some degree of harassment. Dead animals were left on her doorstep more than once. She walked to work every day, and in fact, was never troubled on her journey. After a number of years she was preparing to leave when one of the local women she had been acquainted with asked her a question. "Who is that tall man you walk to work with" she asked, "is he your brother". Our friend had never been aware that she had walked with anyone, but immediately understood the divine protection she had been given.

The fact is, he is longing for us to trust him and put that trust into action. Some years ago James, our youngest son, had started work for our church, Frontline, Liverpool, as a fundraiser. His target was to raise £32,000 in the year. As his parents we made this a faith target. Then one day, within a few weeks of starting, I felt God say to me, "if you believe I can do this in 12 months, why not ask me to do it in 6? So we did. The six months would run until 31st December. By early October only 4 or 5 thousand pounds had come in. By November it was 12 thousand. To be fair,

Five loaves and two fishes

James had done really well to raise this much so quickly. But still we prayed. As December arrived the sum exceeded £20,000 and we became more fervent! By Christmas it was £28,000 and the church offices were then closed for the holiday. We were puzzled why God would allow us to be so close! On January 2nd, as James returned to work, cheques to the value of £4,000 were waiting in his post, all written before December 31st! The £32,000 target was reached!

The story is told of the mouse who befriended an elephant. One day the mouse was sitting on an elephant's back. The mouse asked the elephant to cross a bridge and when they had crossed he said "Wasn't it great how we made that bridge swing!" Of course the word 'we' was not strictly accurate. But that's exactly how God wants us to feel with him. It does feel to us mice that we are taking big risks with God to get God's stuff done. Money risks. Time risks. Love risks. Career risks. Whatever risk we take, when we hear from him, and get involved in his work, it is not really a risk at all. And, like the elephant, God loves to hear us say how exciting it all was!

What is the mountain in your life? A desperately painful background, a character flaw, an awful work situation, a heart breaking family, a broken marriage, a physical illness, a financial burden that seems

Five loaves and two fishes

insurmountable. Whatever it is, you have probably told God about it a hundred times. Or more.

Instead, focus on the mountain mover, not the mountain. Walk with the mountain mover. Take risks with the mountain mover. And enjoy the God of miracles! But remember to do so, you must be ready to part with your loaves and your fishes.

Five loaves and two fishes

Endnotes

---

[i] It is recorded in Matthew 14, Mark 6, Luke 9 and John 6
[ii] Luke 9:10
[iii] John 6:2
[iv] Mark 6:34
[v] Luke 9:11
[vi] Luke 9:13
[vii] Numbers 13:1-end, Numbers 14:1-9
[viii] 1 Samuel 17
[ix] 1 Samuel 16
[x] Mark 6:38
[xi] John 6:8&9
[xii] John 6:11
[xiii] John 3:34
[xiv] In "Multiplying Missional Leaders" (2012) Mike Breen, Pub: 3 Dimensional Ministries

Printed in Great Britain
by Amazon